First World War

and Army of Occupation

War Diary

France, Belgium and Germany

14 DIVISION
Headquarters, Branches and Services
Commander Royal Engineers
19 May 1915 - 20 April 1919

WO95/1884/2

The Naval & Military Press Ltd
www.nmarchive.com
Published in association with The National Archives

Published by

The Naval & Military Press Ltd

Unit 10 Ridgewood Industrial Park,

Uckfield, East Sussex,

TN22 5QE England

Tel: +44 (0) 1825 749494

www.naval-military-press.com

www.nmarchive.com

This diary has been reprinted in facsimile from the original. Any imperfections are inevitably reproduced and the quality may fall short of modern type and cartographic standards.

Contents

Document type	Place/Title	Date From	Date To
War Diary	Tourcoing	01/12/1916	31/12/1916
Heading	A.D.M.S., 14th Division. War Diary. 1st January 1919. To 31st January 1919		
War Diary	Tourcoing	01/01/1919	31/01/1919
Heading	14th Division. War Diary-A.D.M.S., 14th Division Period:- 1/2/19. 28/2/19		
War Diary	Tourcoing	01/02/1919	28/02/1919
Heading	A.D.M.S. 14th Div		
War Diary	Tourcoing	01/03/1919	24/03/1919
Heading	1884/2 1915 May-14th Division 1919 April Commander Royal Engineers		
Heading	14th Division C.R.E. May 1915-Apl 1919		
Heading	H.Q. 14th Div CRE Vol I May to Oct 15		
Heading	War Diary Of CRE 14th Divn From 19th May To 31st Oct 1915		
War Diary	Watten	19/05/1915	22/05/1915
War Diary	Steenvorde	27/05/1915	27/05/1915
War Diary	Vlamertinghe	28/05/1915	13/06/1915
War Diary	IM Ned Abeele	13/06/1915	19/06/1915
War Diary	Vlamertinghe	12/07/1915	31/10/1915
Heading	CRE 14th Div Vol 2		
War Diary		01/11/1915	30/11/1915
Heading	CRE 14th Div Vol 3		
War Diary		01/12/1915	31/12/1915
Miscellaneous	CRE	21/12/1915	21/12/1915
Miscellaneous	Headquarters 14th Divisional Engineers	20/12/1915	20/12/1915
Miscellaneous		19/12/1915	19/12/1915
Miscellaneous			
Miscellaneous	Nominal Roll 62nd Fld Coy R.E		
Miscellaneous	Nominal Roll 89th Field Co. R.E		
Miscellaneous	89th Field Co. R.E.		
Miscellaneous	Nominal Roll Of 14th Signal Company		
Heading	CRE 14th Div Vol 4		
Heading	War Diary Of C.R.E 14th Divn From 1-1-16 To 31-1-16		
War Diary		01/01/1916	31/01/1916
Heading	CRE 14th Div Vol 5		
Heading	War Diary Of C.R.E 14th Division From 1st Feby To 29th Feby 16		
War Diary		01/02/1916	29/02/1916
Heading	War Diary Of C.R.E. 14th Division From 1st March 16 To 31st March 16 C.R.E. 14 Div Vol 6		
War Diary	Dainville	01/03/1916	31/03/1916
Heading	War Diary Of C.R.E. 14th Divn From 1/4/16 To 30/4/16		
War Diary	Dainville	01/04/1916	30/04/1916
Miscellaneous	DAG	02/01/1916	02/01/1916
Miscellaneous	Dainville	01/05/1916	01/05/1916
Miscellaneous	DAG	09/07/1916	09/07/1916
War Diary	Dainville	01/06/1916	18/06/1916

War Diary		17/06/1916	30/06/1916
Heading	War Diaries of C.R.E 14th Division 61st 62nd & 89th Field Companies R.E., From 1st July 16 To 31st July 16		
War Diary	Dainville	01/07/1916	07/07/1916
War Diary	Briqueterie Near Warlus	08/07/1916	30/07/1916
War Diary	Sus. St. Leger	31/07/1916	31/07/1916
Miscellaneous	Consolidation of points during an Attack	27/07/1916	27/07/1916
Heading	14 CRE Vol II 9,61 Volume War Diary Of Headquarters Royal Engineers 14th (Light) Division		
War Diary	Bealcourt	01/08/1916	01/08/1916
War Diary	Bernaville	01/08/1916	07/08/1916
War Diary	Buire Sur L'ancre	08/08/1916	13/08/1916
War Diary	Bellevue Farm	14/08/1916	31/08/1916
Miscellaneous	O.C. 51st Fd Co. R.E	17/08/1916	17/08/1916
Operation(al) Order(s)	14th Division R.E Operation Order No. 5	19/08/1916	19/08/1916
Map	Map No. X 12a		
Map	Map No. X 12b		
Map	Map No. X 19		
Map			
Miscellaneous	A Form. Messages And Signals.		
Miscellaneous	O.C. 89th Field Co. R.E		
Diagram etc			
Miscellaneous		19/08/1916	19/08/1916
Diagram etc			
Diagram etc	Sketch Of St Mars		
Miscellaneous	C.R.E	19/08/1916	19/08/1916
Miscellaneous	A.A. & Q.M.G. 14th Divn	02/10/1916	02/10/1916
Heading	War Diary. of 14th Divisional Engineers For September 1st 1916 to September 30th		
War Diary	Belloy St Laurent	01/09/1916	11/09/1916
War Diary	Buire	12/09/1916	13/09/1916
War Diary	Fricourt	14/09/1916	17/09/1916
War Diary	Buire	18/09/1916	22/09/1916
War Diary	Le Cauroy	23/09/1916	26/09/1916
War Diary	Couy	27/09/1916	28/09/1916
War Diary	Warlus	29/09/1916	30/09/1916
Heading	War Diary Of 14th Divisional Engineers From 1st Oct 16 To 31st Oct 16		
War Diary	Warlus	01/10/1916	31/10/1916
Heading	War Diary Of Headquarters 14th Div Engineer From 1st November 16 To 30th November 1916 Volume I		
War Diary	Warlus	01/11/1916	05/11/1916
War Diary	Couy	06/11/1916	07/11/1916
War Diary	Le Cauroy	08/11/1916	19/12/1916
War Diary	Warlus	19/12/1916	31/12/1916
Heading	War Diaries Of C.R.E. 14th Divn. 61st 62nd & 89th Fd Cos' R.E. From 1.1.17 To 31.1.17		
War Diary	Warlus	01/01/1917	28/02/1917
Heading	War Diaries Of H.Q. 14th Divl Engineers, From/1st March 17 To 31st March 17		
War Diary	Warlus	01/03/1917	31/03/1917
Heading	War Diaries CRE 14th Divn April 1917		
Miscellaneous	AA Q.M.G 14th Div	05/05/1917	05/05/1917
War Diary	Warlus	01/04/1917	24/04/1917
War Diary	Bailleulmont	25/04/1917	26/04/1917
War Diary	N7d. 44	27/04/1917	30/04/1917

Miscellaneous	A.A. & Q.M.G. 14th (Light) Division.	04/06/1917	04/06/1917
Heading	War Diaries 14th Divisional Engineers. Volume Ia. Month Of May 1917		
War Diary	Sheet 51a N7d. 44	01/05/1917	18/05/1917
War Diary	M23 A 7.5	19/05/1917	31/05/1917
Miscellaneous	14th Division "A"	01/07/1917	01/07/1917
Heading	War Diary Headquarters 14th Divisional Engineers. Volume Ib. June 1917		
War Diary	M23a 75 Sheet 51b	01/06/1917	30/06/1917
Miscellaneous	A 14th (Light) Division.	01/08/1917	01/08/1917
War Diary		01/07/1917	28/07/1917
War Diary	Scherpenberg	29/07/1917	29/07/1917
War Diary	Wytschaete	30/07/1917	30/07/1917
War Diary	Locre	31/07/1917	31/07/1917
Heading	War Diaries Of 14th Divisional Engineers From 1st August 1917 To 31st August 1917		
War Diary	Locre	01/08/1917	09/08/1917
War Diary	Belgium	13/08/1917	14/08/1917
War Diary	Reninghelst	15/08/1917	18/08/1917
War Diary	Dickebush	18/08/1917	31/08/1917
War Diary	Berthen	01/09/1917	02/09/1917
War Diary	Ravelberg	03/09/1917	04/09/1917
War Diary	Messines And Gapard	05/09/1917	30/09/1917
Heading	War Diary of 14th Divisional Engineers. From 1st October 1917 To 31st October 1917		
War Diary	Ravelsberg	01/10/1917	31/10/1917
Miscellaneous	Chief Engineer Xth Corps.	05/11/1917	05/11/1917
War Diary	Berthen	01/11/1917	18/11/1917
War Diary	Vlamertinghe	18/11/1917	23/11/1917
War Diary	Belgium	23/11/1917	30/11/1917
War Diary	Vlamertinghe	01/12/1917	02/12/1917
War Diary	Ypres	03/12/1917	31/12/1917
War Diary	Vlamertinghe	01/01/1918	03/01/1918
War Diary	Mericourt Sur-Somme	04/01/1918	24/01/1918
War Diary	Guiscard	25/01/1918	31/01/1918
Miscellaneous	14th Division. No. S.G. 156	23/01/1918	23/01/1918
War Diary	Clastres	01/02/1918	28/02/1918
Heading	14th Divisional Engineers. C.R.E. 14th Division March 1918		
War Diary	Clastres	01/03/1918	21/03/1918
War Diary	Petit Detroit	22/03/1918	31/03/1918
Miscellaneous	Report On Work Of R.E. in The Period 21st, March To 6th. April		
Miscellaneous	Destruction of Bridges Over Crozat Canal		
Heading	War Diary Headquarters. Royal Engineers, 14th Division. April 1918		
War Diary	Hebecourt	01/04/1918	02/04/1918
War Diary	Boyes	02/04/1918	05/04/1918
War Diary	Glissy	06/04/1918	07/04/1918
War Diary	St Fuscien	08/04/1918	10/04/1918
War Diary	Feuquieres	11/04/1918	11/04/1918
War Diary	Hucrheliers	12/04/1918	15/04/1918
War Diary	Ecquedecques	15/04/1918	22/04/1918
War Diary	Coyecque	22/04/1918	28/04/1918
War Diary	Mollinghem	29/04/1918	08/05/1918
War Diary	St Quentin	10/05/1918	31/05/1918

Diagram etc	Breastworks & Bridge Span 25.0		
Miscellaneous	14 Inf Div "O"	02/07/1918	02/07/1918
Miscellaneous	14th Div "B" Forwarded	15/07/1918	15/07/1918
War Diary	St Quentin	01/06/1918	11/07/1918
War Diary	Clarmarais	12/09/1918	12/09/1918
War Diary	Cassel	14/07/1918	12/08/1918
War Diary	Eperlecques	13/08/1918	20/08/1918
War Diary	Chateau Couthove	20/08/1918	19/09/1918
War Diary	Crwell Camp	20/09/1918	27/09/1918
War Diary	Haguefarn	29/09/1918	01/10/1918
War Diary	Busse Boom	02/10/1918	02/10/1918
War Diary	Kandahar Fm	03/10/1918	18/10/1918
War Diary	Chau Hazebrouck Q 31.c	19/10/1918	19/10/1918
War Diary	Blanc Four	19/10/1918	20/10/1918
War Diary	Muscron	21/10/1918	01/11/1918
War Diary	Tourcoing	04/11/1918	20/04/1919

Army Form C. 2118.

WAR DIARY
or
INTELLIGENCE SUMMARY.
(Erase heading not required.)

Instructions regarding War Diaries and Intelligence Summaries are contained in F. S. Regs., Part II. and the Staff Manual respectively. Title pages will be prepared in manuscript.

Place	Date	Hour	Summary of Events and Information	Remarks and references to Appendices
TOURCOING	1/12/18		Visited 44th F Amb.	APS
"	2/12/18		Routine duties. Lt J G. LOUDEN evacuated sick and struck off strength.	APS
"	3/12/18		Routine duties. Capt RIDDELL 44th F Amb detailed to report to Adastral House and struck off strength.	APS
"	4/12/18		Routine duties.	APS
"	5/12/18		Lt HATFIELD M.O.R.C. detailed to proceed for duty with 1st Cavalry Division and struck off strength.	APS
"	6/12/18		Routine duties	APS
"	7/12/18		Visited 44th F Amb.	APS
"	8/12/18		Routine duties	APS
"	9/12/18		Visited 43rd F Amb. Inspected billets of units of 41st Inf Bde. Owing to shortage of MOs MO 14th MG Bn withdrawn and sick ordered to attend at F Amb. which was placed in medical charge of unit.	APS
"	10/12/18		Major B H BARTON MC 44th F Amb and Lt H.S. HOGG i/c 10th HLI ordered to report to Adastral House and struck off strength. 47th Bde RFA placed under charge of 44th F Amb and MO withdrawn for duty with 44 F Amb.	APS
"	11/12/18		Routine duties.	APS
"	12/12/18		Capt R S WOODS 42nd F Amb transferred to Home Establishment. Capt W.H. Shepherd MO 14th Div RE withdrawn to 42nd F Amb and RE placed under charge of F Ambs.	APS
"	13/12/18		Visited 43rd F Amb at PENSIONNAT DE MARCQ (36/K6d)	APS
"	14/12/18		attended first meeting of XV Corps Medical Society	APS
"	15/12/18		Visited HQ 43rd Inf Bde.	APS

D. D. & L., London, E.C. (A8001) Wt. W1-71/M2031 750,000 5/17 Sch. 52 Forms/C2118/14

Instructions regarding War Diaries and Intelligence Summaries are contained in F. S. Regs., Part II. and the Staff Manual respectively. Title pages will be prepared in manuscript.

WAR DIARY
or
INTELLIGENCE SUMMARY.
(Erase heading not required.)

Army Form C. 2118.

Place	Date	Hour	Summary of Events and Information	Remarks and references to Appendices
TOURCOING	16/12/18		Routine duties	APS
"	17/12/18		Routine duties	APS
"	18/12/18		Lt. N.T. JOHNSON M.O.R.C reported for duty and posted to 42nd F Amb.	APS
"	19/12/18		Representative RAMC team of Division defeated 47th Bde R.F.A. by 10 goals to nil in the final of the Divisional association league.	APS
"	20/12/18		Routine duties.	APS
"	21/12/18		Routine duties	APS
"	22/12/18		Routine duties.	APS
"	23/12/18		attended G.O.C.'s Conference at Divl HQ. re Louse and other problems.	APS
"	24/12/18		attended Conference at D.D.M.S office.	APS
"	25/12/18		Xmas duties	APS
"			Lt JOHNSON 42nd F Amb sick in hospital. AD. visited DRStn and 43rd F Amb	APS
"	26/12/18		Lt BROWNING att^d 14th MGC sent for duty with No 5 Labour Group. Capt DODS 43rd F Amb sent to replace Lt BROWNING.	APS
"	27/12/18			APS
"	28/12/18.		Routine duties	APS
"	29/12/18		Routine duties.	APS
"	30/12/18.		Routine duties — R. Thomson Capt. RAMC	
"	31/12/18.		Routine duties — R. Thomson Capt RAMC	

R. Thomson Capt RAMC
for A.D. MS 14th Div.

D. D. & L., London, E.C.
(A8001) Wt. W1271/M2031 750,000 5/17 Sch. 52 Forms/C2118/14

Jan. 1919

VR 42

A.D.M.S., 14th Division.

****

WAR DIARY.

*** *****

140/3489

1st January 1919. to 31st January 1919.

v***************************************

Box 1584

3/2/19.

Army Form C. 2118.

Instructions regarding War Diaries and Intelligence Summaries are contained in F. S. Regs., Part II. and the Staff Manual respectively. Title pages will be prepared in manuscript.

WAR DIARY
or
INTELLIGENCE SUMMARY.
(Erase heading not required.)

Place	Date	Hour	Summary of Events and Information	Remarks and references to Appendices
TOURCOING	1/1/19.		Festive duties	A. Thomson Capt RAMC
"	2/1/19		Routine duties. 2 O.R. Sent home for demobilization	NM
"	3/1/19		Visited 42nd F.A. and 44th F.A.	NM
"	4/1/19		Routine duties	NM
"	5/1/19.		" 6 O.R. demobilized	NM
"	6/1/19.		Routine duties.	NM
"	7/1/19		do	NM
"	8/1/19		do 1. O.R. demobilized	NM
"	9/1/19		do	NM
"	10/1/19		do	NM
"	11/1/19		do 4. O.R. demobilized	NM
"	12/1/19		A.D.M.S. attended Medical Soc. meeting XV Corps. 8. O.R. Demobilized.	NM
"	13/1/19		Major Saint D.A.D.M.S. proceeded on leave. 8 O.R. Demobilized	NM
"	14/1/19		Routine duties	NM
"	15/1/19		do.	NM
"	16/1/19.		The A.D.M.S. held a conference of F.A. Commanders to consider the question of Demobilization of RAMC The D.A.D.M.S. XV Corps attended.	NM
"	17/1/19.		Routine duties	NM
"	18/1/19		" 22. O.R. Demobilized	NM
"	19/1/19		" 22 O.R. "	NM
"	20/1/19		" 18. O.R. "	NM
"	21/1/19		" 9 O.R. "	NM
"	22/1/19		" 13. O.R. "	NM.

D. D. & L., London, E.C.
(A8001) Wt. W1771/M2031 750,000 5/17 Sch. 52 Forms/C2.118/14

Army Form C. 2118.

Instructions regarding War Diaries and Intelligence Summaries are contained in F. S. Regs., Part II. and the Staff Manual respectively. Title pages will be prepared in manuscript.

WAR DIARY
or
INTELLIGENCE SUMMARY.

(Erase heading not required.)

Place	Date	Hour	Summary of Events and Information	Remarks and references to Appendices
			R. Thomson Capt RAMC	
TURCOING	23/1/19		Routine Duties	
"	24/1/19		Colonel CAMPBELL DSO proceeded on leave to U.K. Lt Col. Egan DSO. 44th F.A took over duties of A.D.M.S.	
"	25/1/19		The A.D.M.S. attends XI Corps. Medical Society meeting	
"	26/1/19		Routine duties	
"	27/1/19		do	
"	28/1/19		do	
"	29/1/19		Lt Col. Egan DSO proceeded on leave to U.K. Lt Col. Evans D.SO 43rd F.A. took over duties of A.D.MS	
"	30/1/19		Routine duties	
"	31/1/19		Routine duties	

R. Thomson
Capt RAMC
for A.D.M.S. XIV Division

D. D. & L., London, E.C.
(A8001) Wt. W1771/M2031 750,000 5/17 Sch. 52 Forms/C2118/14

140/3526

14th DIVISION.
****

WAR DIARY. - A.D.M.S., 14th DIVISION.
*** ****** **** **************

Period:- 1/2/19. - 28/2/19.

1/3/19.

Army Form C. 2118.

WAR DIARY
or
INTELLIGENCE SUMMARY.
(Erase heading not required.)

Instructions regarding War Diaries and Intelligence Summaries are contained in F. S. Regs., Part II. and the Staff Manual respectively. Title pages will be prepared in manuscript.

Place	Date	Hour	Summary of Events and Information	Remarks and references to Appendices
TOURCOING	1/2/19		Routine duties	APS
"	2/2/19		"	APS
"	3/2/19		DADMS returned from leave	APS
"	4/2/19		Routine duties	APS
"	5/2/19		4 ORs demobilised	APS
"	6/2/19		Visited 44th F Amb	APS
"	7/2/19		Visited 43rd F Amb. Capt P. LASKARI IMS reported for duty and taken on strength of 44th F Amb.	APS
"	8/2/19		4 ORs demobilised	APS
"	9/2/19		ADMS returned from leave. 4 ORs demobilised.	APS
"	10/2/19		4 ORs demobilised. Major DUNLOP 43rd F Amb took over tempy command of 43rd F Amb during absence of O.C. of that unit	APS
"	11/2/19		Routine duties	APS
"	12/2/19		Visited 43rd F Amb	APS
"	13/2/19		6 ORs demobilised. Lt Browning MORC proceeded for temporary duty with No 10. CC Stn	APS
"	14/2/19		6 ORs demobilised.	APS
"	15/2/19		6 ORs demobilised	APS
"	16/2/19		6 ORs demobilised	APS
"	17/2/19		6 ORs demobilised	APS

D. D. & L., London, E.C. (A8001) Wt. W1-71/M2031 750,000 5/17 Sch. 52 Forms/C2118/14

Instructions regarding War Diaries and Intelligence Summaries are contained in F. S. Regs., Part II. and the Staff Manual respectively. Title pages will be prepared in manuscript.

WAR DIARY
or
INTELLIGENCE SUMMARY.
(Erase heading not required.)

Army Form C. 2118.

Place	Date	Hour	Summary of Events and Information	Remarks and references to Appendices
TOURCOING	18/2/19		T/Capt N.M. RANKIN 42nd F Amb proceeded to U.K for demobilisation and struck off strength	ADS
"	19/2/19		Visited 42nd F Amb	ADS
"	20/2/19		6 ORs demobilised	ADS
"	21/2/19		6 ORs demobilised. Visited 44th F Amb.	ADS
"	22/2/19		6 ORs demobilised.	ADS
"	23/2/19		6 ORs demobilised	ADS
"	24/2/19		Visited 44th F Amb. 6 ORs demobilised	ADS
"	25/2/19		T/Capt (Maj) D.S. GRAHAM 44th F Amb proceeded to report to Adastral House on expiration of contract. T/Capt D C WELSH 44th F Amb. proceeded to U.K for demobilisation and struck off strength	ADS
"	26/2/19		Routine duties.	ADS
"	27/2/19		6 ORs demobilised.	ADS
"	28/2/19		6 ORs demobilised. T/Capt H.F. STEPHENS 14th DAC proceeded to take over Command of 14th M.A.C Total Ration Strength of Division now 4910	ADS

A D Saint Major RAMC
DADMS
14th Div

D. D. & L., London, E.C.
(A8001) Wt. W1-71/M2031 750,000 5/17 Sch. 52 Forms/C2118/14

Mar. 1919.

160/3553.

A.D.M.S. 14th Div.

Instructions regarding War Diaries and Intelligence Summaries are contained in F. S. Regs., Part II. and the Staff Manual respectively. Title pages will be prepared in manuscript.

WAR DIARY
or
INTELLIGENCE SUMMARY.
(*Erase heading not required.*)

Army Form C. 2118.

Vol 44

Place	Date	Hour	Summary of Events and Information	Remarks and references to Appendices
TOURCOING	1/3/19		Visited DDMS XVth Corps	ABS
"	2/3/19		Routine duties.	ABS
"	3/3/19		T/Capt. J.A. CONWAY proceeded to U.K. for demobilisation	ABS
"	4/3/19		Routine duties	ABS
"	5/3/19		Visited 44th F Amb.	ABS
"	6/3/19		9 ORs demobilised.	ABS
"	7/3/19		9 ORs demobilised.	ABS
"	8/3/19		9 O.R.s demobilised	PJK
"	9/3/19		9 O.Rs demobilised	PJK
"	10/3/19		9 O.Rs demobilised	PJK
"	11/3/19		Routine duties	
"	12/3/19		Routine duties.	PJK
"	13/3/19		MAJ. W. EGAN. D.S.O. proceeded to United Kingdom for service in India 12/3/19. and struck off the strength. 9 O.Rs demobilised. CAPT. A.E. WEBSTER. M.C. and CAPT. R.L. WOOD proceeded for demobilisation and struck off the strength	PJK
"	14/3/19		9 O.Rs demobilised	PJK
	15/3/19		CAPT. A.P. SAINT. M.C. and CAPT. M.J. KELLY proceeded to COLOGNE to report to D.M.S. Second Army and struck off the strength. 9 O.Rs demobilised.	PJK

D. D. & L., London, E.C.
(A8031) Wt. W1-71/M2031 750,000 5/17 Sch. 52 Forms/C2118/14

Army Form C. 2118.

Instructions regarding War Diaries and Intelligence Summaries are contained in F. S. Regs., Part II. and the Staff Manual respectively. Title pages will be prepared in manuscript.

WAR DIARY
or
INTELLIGENCE SUMMARY.
(Erase heading not required.)

Place	Date	Hour	Summary of Events and Information	Remarks and references to Appendices
TOURCOING	16/3/19	-	LT. COL. S. H. CAMPBELL. D.S.O. proceeded to the United Kingdom for service in India and struck off the strength	
			CAPT. W. H. SHEPHARD proceeded for demobilisation and is struck off the strength.	
			CAPT. & LT. COL. C. HELM. D.S.O. M.C. took over duties of Act A.D.M.S.	
			4 O.R.s demobilised	C.H.
"	17/3/19	-	4. O.R.S. demobilised. D.D.M.S. XVth Corps visited A.D.M.S.	C.H.
"	18/3/19	-	A.D.M.S. visited D.D.M.S. XVth Corps	C.H.
"	19/3/19	-	Routine duties	C.H.
"	20/3/19	-	CAPT. G. S. L. KEMP and sixteen O.R.s proceeded to join the Armies of the Rhine.	C.H.
			4. O.R.s demobilised.	C.H.
"	21/3/19	-	Routine duties	C.H.
"	22/3/19	-	6. O.R.s were transferred to 62. C.C.S.	
			4. O.R.s proceeded for demobilisation	C.H.
"	23/3/19	-	CAPT. THOMPSON proceeded to Second Army COLOGNE and is struck off the strength.	
			4. O.R.s proceeded for demobilisation	C.H.
	24/3/19	-	1. O.R. proceeded for demobilisation.	
			A.D.M.S. office 14th DIV. closes at noon to-day. In accordance with the new Army Administration there is no longer an A.D.M.S. at Div. Hqs.	
			C. Helm Lt. Col.	
			O/A.D.M.S. 14th DIV.	

D. D. & L., London, E.C.
(A8093) Wt. W1 71/M2031 750,000 5/17 Sch. 52 Forms/C2118/14

1884/2

1915 May –
1919 April

14th Division
Commander Royal
Engineers

14TH DIVISION

C. R. E.

MAY 1915-APL 1919

K

H.Q. 14th Div: C.R.E.

Vol I

May to Oct 15

– Apl '19

A.G.
Base

CONFIDENTIAL

War Diary
of
CRE 14th Divn

From 19th May to 31st Oct 1915.

Army Form C. 2118.

Instructions regarding War Diaries and Intelligence Summaries are contained in F. S. Regs., Part II. and the Staff Manual respectively. Title pages will be prepared in manuscript.

WAR DIARY

or

~~INTELLIGENCE SUMMARY.~~

(Erase heading not required.)

Place	Date	Hour	Summary of Events and Information	Remarks and references to Appendices
ALDERSHOT	19/5/15	4.50am	Left Aldershot.	
WATTEN	22nd	5.pm	Arrived WATTEN.	
STEENVORDE	27th	2.0PM	Marched to STEENVOORDE.	
VLAMERTINGHE	28/5	12.0N.	" " VLAMERTINGHE	
	29/5 to 5/6	9.0AM	At VLAMERTINGHE: 61st Coy employed on Ramparts at YPRES; 62nd & 89th Coy on supporting points in ELVERDINGHE switch	
	5/6	9.0AM	Marched to WESTOUTRE	
	5/6 to 13/6		At WESTOUTRE. 61st Coy at DICKEBUSCH, working in front trenches; 62nd " at LA CLYTTE, working on GHQ 3 under CRE 46th Div.; 89th " at DRANOUTRE " " " CE 2nd Corps.	
1 M. W. of ABEELE	13/6 to 19/6	9.30 AM	Marched to 1 M West of ABEELE. 62nd & 89th Coys march to same neighbourhood. At do. do. On 16th, 62nd Coy, with 42nd Bde. in reserve for attack on german trenches N. of HOOGE. Maj. R.A. Gillam wounded.	
	19/6	2.0PM	Marched to ½ M. West of VLAMERTINGHE	
	19/6 to		In billet at do do do Conducting Operations E of YPRES	
			19/20 – 42nd Infy. Bde & 62 Co. R.E. took over portion of front line from 3rd Division	
VLAMERTINGHE	12/7		Bt-Lt-Col. A.J. Sargeaunt RE took over duties of CRE from Lt Col H Prentice.	
		9.30am	CRE met C.E. VI Corps at 42nd Bde H.Q., & visited work at Chateau I9d & I10c afterwards CRE visited front trenches.	
	13th	9am	Visited supporting points ~~S.E~~ in H 10 c & d.	
	~~14th~~	2pm	" Liverpools workshops in YPRES.	
	14th	9am	" Trenches with G.O.C.	
	~~15th~~			

1577 Wt. W10791/1773 500,000 1/15 D. D. & L. A.D.S.S./Forms/C. 2118.

Army Form C. 2118.

Instructions regarding War Diaries and Intelligence Summaries are contained in F. S. Regs., Part II. and the Staff Manual respectively. Title pages will be prepared in manuscript.

WAR DIARY
or
~~INTELLIGENCE SUMMARY.~~
(Erase heading not required.)

Place	Date	Hour	Summary of Events and Information	Remarks and references to Appendices
	July 15th		62nd Coy took over work in front trenches from 61st Coy.	
			61st " " " " at supporting points in H 10 c & d & I 9 d from 62nd Coy	
			89th continued work on communication trenches, with two Coys. Liverpools.	
	20th		Visited front trenches.	
	21st		" trenches occupied by 8th Bde, near HOOGE & SANCTUARY WOOD, with C R E 3rd Division	
			Capt. K W Pye injured, & sent to base.	
	21st–22nd		14th Div. came in 6th Corps.	
			61st Coy, with 41st Bde., took over sector G, from 8th Bde.	
			62nd Coy remain ~~with~~ in sector H.	
			These two coys. responsible for all RE work back to GHQ 2. One Coy. of Liverpools at disposal of each.	
			89th Coy. at WHITE CHATEAU, ECOLE, & H 10 c & d.	
	23rd		Capt. Chesney assumed temporary command of 62nd Coy.	
	24th		Visited trenches at HOOGE with G. S. O. 1	
			2Lt O. D. M. Christie arrived – 62nd Coy.	
	26th		Lt. A D C Fenwick " 61st "	
			~~A huts~~ Started removing 'A' huts from H 9 a to H 1 b, by Belgian labour	

1577 Wt. W10791/1773 500,000 1/15 D. D. & L. A.D.S.S./Forms/C. 2118.

Instructions regarding War Diaries and Intelligence Summaries are contained in F. S. Regs., Part II. and the Staff Manual respectively. Title pages will be prepared in manuscript.

WAR DIARY

or

~~INTELLIGENCE SUMMARY.~~

(Erase heading not required.)

Army Form C. 2118.

Place	Date	Hour	Summary of Events and Information	Remarks and references to Appendices
	July 22 onwards.		RE work of all kinds being much hindered by lack of material, principally 1 inch boarding, nails, & corrugated iron & roofing felt.	
	28		Visited trenches at HOOGE.	
	29		" supporting points at H 10 c & d.	
	30	2.30 am	Trenches near HOOGE captured by Germans.	
		2 pm	Counter attack, which failed.	
	31st	1 pm	Lt-Col. A. J. Sargeaunt killed by shell near ZILLEBEKE Major J. P. Mackesy R.E. assumed duties of CRE.	
	30th		~~Adt~~ Garrett Smith wounded.	
	31st		Lt. Paddison wounded.	
	Aug. 1		2 Sections 59th Coy relieved ~~two~~ sections 61st Coy at SANCTUARY Wood.	
	~~4~~		Lt. M. C. Crompton wounded.	
	4.		Lt-Col. T.A.H. Biggs arrived, & assumed duties of CRE	
	5-6.		16th Inf. Bde relieved 42nd & 43rd Bdes, from southern end of Y wood to SANCTUARY wood. G.O.C. 6th Div. took command of this sector on completion of relief. 59th Coy. relieved by 1st London Fd. Coy.	
	6		CRE visited H sector trenches with Maj. Mackesy & Capt. Chesney.	

1577 Wt. W10791/1773 500,000 1/15 D. D. & L. A.D.S.S./Forms/C. 2118.

Army Form C. 2118.

Instructions regarding War Diaries and Intelligence Summaries are contained in F. S. Regs., Part II. and the Staff Manual respectively. Title pages will be prepared in manuscript.

WAR DIARY
or
INTELLIGENCE SUMMARY.
(Erase heading not required.)

Place	Date	Hour	Summary of Events and Information	Remarks and references to Appendices
	Aug. 7	10.30 am	Conference of O.C. Coys. with C.R.E. The following distribution of work was decided on. (a) 89th Coy. to take over work in 'H' sector, with 42nd Bde, from 62nd Coy. To do work in front & support trenches; line of supporting points behind support line – conversion of saps from H16. H17. H18 into fire trench. construction of listening galleries (b) 62nd Coy to work in G.H.Q. 2 (machine gun emplacements) White Chateau (take over from 89th Coy) & various jobs in YPRES. (c) 61st Coy. to work on rear supporting points, & general work W. of YPRES. (d) 11/dive pools continue working on main communication trenches.	
	9		above reliefs & distribution of work commenced.	
	10		~~1 NCO & 6 men ordered to go to Cornwalls' Workshops at ABEELE to make trench tramways~~ Cancelled.	
	10		43rd Bde relieved 42nd Bde in H sector.	
	13th		61st Coy take over 'A' sector with 41st Inf. Bde. from 56th Coy. & 9th Inf. Bde. 62nd Coy. take over rear supporting points & other jobs W. of YPRES from 61st Coy.	
	11th		3 Brigade Mining Sections, under Capt. C.W. FRENCH, 5/KSLI, started work in H Sector, sinking listening galleries.	

1577 Wt. W10791/1773 500,000 1/15 D. D. & L. A.D.S.S./Forms/C. 2118.

Instructions regarding War Diaries and Intelligence Summaries are contained in F. S. Regs., Part II. and the Staff Manual respectively. Title pages will be prepared in manuscript.

WAR DIARY
or
INTELLIGENCE SUMMARY.
(Erase heading not required.)

Army Form C. 2118.

Place	Date	Hour	Summary of Events and Information	Remarks and references to Appendices
	16	9.45 am	Visited trenches – EAST & WEST LANES, & RAILWAY WOOD.	
	19		62nd Coy relieved 89th Coy in H sector, E. of CAMBRIDGE Rd. 89th Coy took on White Chateau, GHQ 2, & Durham Redoubt. 62nd Coy continue at Somerset Redoubt.	
	20–21		42nd Bde relieved 43rd Bde in H sector.	
	22		Visited trenches – West Lane – front of A sector – HAYMARKET.	
	23		Capt Morgan took command of 62nd Co. vice Capt Chesney on leave, Lt. Fenwick took over duties of Adjutant	
	24		61st Co. continue work in A sector & repairing roads in H.7.a. 62nd in H sector & 89th at WHITE CHATEAU	
	25		~~Schemes~~ for demolition of No 9 bridge, & fougasses at MENIN GATE drawn up by 89th Co. & all preparations made	
	26.		Visited road bridges 1.A. 7. 8. 9. over canal at YPRES.	
	27.		Visited defences of ECOLE, YPRES & line of tramway from MENIN GATE to PRISON in YPRES	
	28		——	
	29		——	

1577 Wt. W10791/1773 500,000 1/15 D. D. & L. A.D.S.S./Forms/C. 2118.

Instructions regarding War Diaries and Intelligence Summaries are contained in F. S. Regs., Part II. and the Staff Manual respectively. Title pages will be prepared in manuscript.

WAR DIARY
or
INTELLIGENCE SUMMARY.
(Erase heading not required.)

Army Form C. 2118.

Place	Date	Hour	Summary of Events and Information	Remarks and references to Appendices
	30.		[illegible] arranged to take over L_4 with French Commandant in charge of BRIELEN works	
	31.		Visited L_4 on YPRES-VLAMERTINGHE ROAD with G.S.O.3 & took over details of works, stores etc from French Engineers. Drew up scheme for completion of work.	
	1.9.15.		Attended conference of C.E. VI corps & drainage expert to deal with drainage of front line trenches occupied by VI corps. 61st Co. prepared Nos 7 & 8 road bridges for demolition	
	2.		Visited works P_1 & P_2 ~~[illegible]~~ E of VLAMERTINGHE. Took over these works from 1st Field Sqdn. R.E. & drew up scheme for completion of work. Visited YPRES about defence of the town ~~[illegible]~~.	
	3		————	
	4		Visited front line trenches in H sector. RAILWAYWOOD & Y WOOD	
	5.		Adjt visited R.E. Park ABEELE & 2nd Army workshops ARMENTIERES to try & get pumps. None available.	
	6.		————	
	7		Went round works P_1 P_2 & L_4	
	8		Visited YPRES for conference with G.O.C. 42nd Inf Bde.	
	9		Adjt. went to HAZEBROUCK & ST OMER to buy nails. Bought 1200 Kilos.	

1577 Wt. W10791/1773 500,000 1/15 D. D. & L. A.D.S.S./Forms/C. 2118.

Instructions regarding War Diaries and Intelligence Summaries are contained in F. S. Regs., Part II. and the Staff Manual respectively. Title pages will be prepared in manuscript.

WAR DIARY
or
INTELLIGENCE SUMMARY.
(*Erase heading not required.*)

Army Form C. 2118.

Place	Date	Hour	Summary of Events and Information	Remarks and references to Appendices
	10.			
	11.		Visited front line trenches in A sector with O.C. 61st Co RE. 89th Co. relieve 62nd Co in front line H. sector.	
	12			
	13		Visited communication trenches up to H. sector	
	~~14~~		Took over KAAIE SALIENT from C.E 6th Corps.	
	~~14~~		Adjt. went to DUNKERQUE & ordered 50 pumps & 100 valves from M. VANDERSLUYS COUDEKERQUE BRANCHE. DUNKERQUE.	
	15.		Went round KAAIE SALIENT	
	16		Went round defences of ÉCOLE nr. YPRES.	
	17		Visited YPRES with G.O.C. 14th Div. to estimate material for house to house defence of the town	
	18.		Estimates of materials for KAAIE SALIENT & house to house defence of YPRES got out.	
	19.			
	20.		Visited trenches with C.E. 6th Corps. Went to see practice operation of 62nd Co & 42nd Inf Bde.	

1577 Wt. W10791/1773 500,000 1/15 D. D. & L. A.D.S.S./Forms/C. 2118.

Instructions regarding War Diaries and Intelligence Summaries are contained in F. S. Regs., Part II. and the Staff Manual respectively. Title pages will be prepared in manuscript.

WAR DIARY
or
INTELLIGENCE SUMMARY.
(Erase heading not required.)

Army Form C. 2118.

Place	Date	Hour	Summary of Events and Information	Remarks and references to Appendices
	21			
	22		Inspection of Cos. by Corps Commander. Adjt went to DUNKERQUE to see about pumps, hose, canvas, oil. Interpreter went to BOULOGNE & CALAIS for pumps & hose	
	23		Inspected 49th Divisional Workshops & Bde Workshops in POPERINGHE	
	24		62nd Co. relieved 89th Co in trenches 42nd Bde relieved 43rd Bde. 2 sections of 61st Co. remain in A sector under 6th Divn	
	25		61st Co. less 2 sections in A sector & 89th Co. remained in Divisional Reserve in H 7 central. During afternoon 1 sec 89th Co. went to Ramparts YPRES. to reinforce 62nd Co.	
	26		Visited front line trenches in H sector. Lieut A.F.M. CLARK, & 2nd Lt BARLERIN 62nd Co wounded.	
	27		89th Co. relieved 62nd Co. in front line H sector.	
	28		Capt BENSKIN O.C. 89th Co. & 2/Lt. D. PERROTT 89th Co. slightly wounded. 2nd Lt. J.T. HALLEY joined 62nd Co. R.E. ~~[illegible]~~	[illegible]
	29		2nd Lt PERROTT sent to 43rd Fd Ambulance	
	30		Visited 41st Bde H.Q. YPRES 2nd Lt GRINDLEY joined 62nd Co 2nd Lt MOWBRAY joined 89th Co.	
	1.		Capt D. FRASER R.E. (T.C.) joined & S.M. REID joined H.Q.	

Oct 15

Instructions regarding War Diaries and Intelligence Summaries are contained in F. S. Regs., Part II. and the Staff Manual respectively. Title pages will be prepared in manuscript.

WAR DIARY
or
INTELLIGENCE SUMMARY.
(Erase heading not required.)

Army Form C. 2118.

Place	Date	Hour	Summary of Events and Information	Remarks and references to Appendices
	2			
	3		Interpreter sent to ST OMER to buy tools & nails	
	4		Visited front line trenches in H Sector with Gen HILL 2nd Lt R.B.PERROTT rejoined. 43rd Bde & 2 sections 89th Co. took over from 50th & 78th Co. Bde nr. VOORMEZEELE ~~[illegible]~~	
	5		Went to ARMENTIERES to purchase stoves, & circular saws.	
	6		Hutting factories practically organized, one Section from Each Coy set aside for this purpose.	
	7		2nd Lt A.W.COOPER joined 89th Co. R.E. Visited Bde Workshops & specimen dugouts	
	8		~~Went~~ Interpreter sent to buy & hire locomobile engine without success.	
	9		Stores taken over by Capt Fraser, who also took over the hutting of the Division	
	10		2/Lt ARC Jenks took over duties of Adjt from Lt CDA FENWICK RE	
	11		about this time the hutting factories had been increased by parties from the	
	12		11th Liverpools, infantry & Belgians (civilian) in all the total employed about 250 in strength	
	13		CAPT PHREIS 89th Coy RE wounded rifle fire VOORMEZEELE	
	14		CRE visited HORNWORK with Capt French. (OC Mining Coy)	
	15		Divisional night working parties resumed. 2 Sections 89th Coy return from St ELOI	
	16		Div. day working parties resumed.	
	17			
	18		GOC 6th Corps visited YPRES with CRE + OC Mining Coy	
	19		Lt HTGRINDLEY 62nd Coy killed near Railway wood by rifle fire	

1577 Wt. W10791/1773 500,000 1/15 D. D. & L. A.D.S.S./Forms/C. 2118.

Army Form C. 2118.

WAR DIARY
or
INTELLIGENCE SUMMARY.
(Erase heading not required.)

Instructions regarding War Diaries and Intelligence Summaries are contained in F. S. Regs., Part II. and the Staff Manual respectively. Title pages will be prepared in manuscript.

Place	Date	Hour	Summary of Events and Information	Remarks and references to Appendices
	20		GOC 6th Corps visited show ground 62nd Coy	
	21 & 22		14th Div relieved by 6th Div & went into rest: RE work handed over to 6th Div, except hutting work	
	25		CRE proceeded to England on leave	
	27		Show ground (Technical School) 62nd Co) inspected by Army Comm & Staff.	
	28		King inspected detachment of troops from 14th Div, including 25 from RE. Major [illegible] a/CRE was present.	
	29		Camps inspected by Maj Gen [illegible] CE 2nd Army	
	31		CRE returned from leave	
	~~1~~		~~Representatives inspected pipe forcing jacks at 6th Corps headqrs~~ [initials]	

[signature] Lt Col CRE

2/11/15

1577 Wt. W10791/1773 500,000 1/15 D. D. & L. A.D.S.S./Forms/C. 2118.

CRE. 14th Div:
Vol: 2

121/7767

Nov. 15

Instructions regarding War Diaries and Intelligence Summaries are contained in F. S. Regs., Part II. and the Staff Manual respectively. Title pages will be prepared in manuscript.

WAR DIARY
or
~~INTELLIGENCE SUMMARY.~~
(*Erase heading not required.*)

November 1915

CRE 14th Div.

Army Form C. 2118.

Place	Date	Hour	Summary of Events and Information	Remarks and references to Appendices
	1 Nov		Representatives visited demonstration of pipe-forcing jacks at 6th Corps Headqrs.	
	2		Reports having been received that hut-building operations near R.E. Camps were becoming very conspicuous, attempts made to screen them.	
	3.		2 Bns 41st I.B. lent to 6th Divn, + 2 to 49th Div, as supports + for work on front line.	
			Interpreters + officers sent every other day or even more frequently to purchase stores such as felt + nails, paint, + accessories for hut building. ~~Haz~~ HAZEBROUCK, BAILLEUL, + even BOULOGNE + CALAIS visited.	
	4 } 5 }		Considerable shortage of stores still apparent - particularly materials for huts	
	8		Battalions ~~[illegible]~~ ordered to practice Winter breastworks: material made by Fd Coys	
	9th onwards		Practise continued.	
	13		CRE visited trenches from I 36 to C 16 C central with CRE 6th Div.	
	14		Conference between CRE + OC Coys on details of organization in new trenches	

1577 Wt. W10791/1773 500,000 1/15 D. D. & L. A.D.S.S./Forms/C. 2118.

Instructions regarding War Diaries and Intelligence Summaries are contained in F. S. Regs., Part II. and the Staff Manual respectively. Title pages will be prepared in manuscript.

Army Form C. 2118.

WAR DIARY
or
~~INTELLIGENCE SUMMARY.~~
(Erase heading not required.)

Nov 1915
CRE 14th Div

Place	Date	Hour	Summary of Events and Information	Remarks and references to Appendices
	16 } 17 }		14th Div relieved 6th Div from I 5 d 6.0 to C 15 c. 2 sections of each Fd Coy to each Brigade in trenches ½ section of each Fd Coy on Hutting for troops in rear.	
	18th & subsequently.		RE's attached to Brigades engaged in reclaiming trenches, which were in a v. bad state owing to ~~[illegible]~~ much rain. Pioneer Battalion engaged in rebuilding main communication trenches, one company to each Brigade, under orders of G.O.C's Bdes. Other Company on various work such as maintenance of ~~[illegible]~~ YPRES ramparts, tramway lines, Divisional workshops &c	
	23rd & subsequently,		Parts of the trenches having been reclaimed, considerable attention now paid to the drainage system, which is now being improved, & to the laying of trench tramways. Large numbers of French Dugout shelters ~~erected~~ being erected by infantry & Belgian civilians under RE supervision.	

1577 Wt. W10791/1773 500,000 1/15 D. D. & L. A.D.S.S./Forms/C. 2118.

Instructions regarding War Diaries and Intelligence Summaries are contained in F. S. Regs., Part II. and the Staff Manual respectively. Title pages will be prepared in manuscript.

WAR DIARY
or
~~INTELLIGENCE SUMMARY.~~
(Erase heading not required.)

CRE 14th Div
Nov. 1915

Army Form C. 2118.

Place	Date	Hour	Summary of Events and Information	Remarks and references to Appendices
	25. onwards		Working parties of about 150 by day + 200 by night attached to right Brigade from 6th Div, for wiring subsidiary line. Additional machine gun emplacements made in support lines.	
	28th		Additional half section per coy attached to Brigades for trench work, making in each Coy – 2½ sections attached to Brigades, ½ section hutting, + 1 section in camp, making trench stores &c. Men of camp section relieving those attached to Brigades periodically	
	29th		Work continues on M/G emplacements, wiring of subsidiary line, drainage of trenches, trolley lines, erection of French dugouts &c. Some breastworks already commenced by 6th Div, continued, + others commenced. One Brigade attached 100 men to its Field Coy for Engineer Work permanently, under orders of O C Fd Coy.	
	30th		Owing to Infantry relief every other night, + bad weather, progress generally slow.	

J M Closs[illegible] Col
CRE

Instructions regarding War Diaries and Intelligence Summaries are contained in F. S. Regs., Part II. and the Staff Manual respectively. Title pages will be prepared in manuscript.

~~WAR~~ DIARY ~~stet~~
or
~~INTELLIGENCE SUMMARY.~~
(Erase heading not required.)

CRE 14th Div

December 1915

Army Form C. 2118.

Place	Date	Hour	Summary of Events and Information	Remarks and references to Appendices
	December.			
	1st		Work in hand as follows:-	
			1 Reclaiming of front line trenches, communication trenches (by Pioneer Battn), Drainage, &c.	
			2 M/G emplacements & wiring in support line, & extra dugouts	
			3 French Dugouts on Canal Bank.	
			4 Trench tramway lines forward from the advanced transport dumps to the trenches & as these become completed, extending back to YPRES to relieve transport	
			5 Making of Trench stores in Workshops &c	
			6 Hutting for troops in rear.	
			7 Repair of bye roads.	
			Working parties of 150 by day & night from 6th Div on the right brigade sector have employed. 100 infantry of the centre sector placed under the orders of the Field Coy commander. Altogether about 300 Belgian civilians employed on Canal Bank (French Dugouts) on roads, in Workshops & on hutting.	

1577 Wt. W10791/1773 500,000 1/15 D. D. & L. A.D.S.S./Forms/C. 2118.

Instructions regarding War Diaries and Intelligence Summaries are contained in F. S. Regs., Part II. and the Staff Manual respectively. Title pages will be prepared in manuscript.

WAR DIARY
or
~~INTELLIGENCE SUMMARY.~~
(Erase heading not required.)

CRE 14th Div

December 1915

Army Form C. 2118.

Place	Date	Hour	Summary of Events and Information	Remarks and references to Appendices
	Dec 1st onwards		Work outlined on previous page continues.	
	2		Pumps supplied to Front line require good deal of maintenance. Dunkerque pump (zinc) found too flimsy. Beck pump with ball valves is best. No pump much use unless it has ball valves, & diaphragm pump preferred to plunger ditto. Insufficient spare parts supplied, especially jointings. Rate of progress on Trolley lines 90x per night if transport sufficient	
	3		Dummy breastworks on part of left sector. Not popular with neighbouring troops	
	7th		Gas emplacements made in technical showground. Subsequently approved by II army gas expert.	
	9		Gabions of expanded metal found to be quite successful for revetments: these & "box" hurdles are the only things of much use	
	15th & 16th		14th Div relieved in the line by 6th Div & ordered to get ready to move	
	17th		Hutting handed over to CE sixth Corps.	

1577 Wt. W10791/1773 500,000 1/15 D. D. & L. A.D.S.S./Forms/C. 2118.

Instructions regarding War Diaries and Intelligence Summaries are contained in F. S. Regs., Part II. and the Staff Manual respectively. Title pages will be prepared in manuscript.

WAR DIARY
or
~~INTELLIGENCE SUMMARY.~~
(Erase heading not required.)

CRE 14th Div
Dec 1915

Army Form C. 2118.

Place	Date	Hour	Summary of Events and Information	Remarks and references to Appendices
	18th-25th		time spent by Fd Coys in preparing to move. Winter clothing handed in.	
	19th		Hutting handed over by CE sixth Corps to CRE 14th Div again.	
	20		Lt Col TAH Biggs to CRE 6th Div. Lt Col F.M. Close assumes duties of CRE 14th Div.	
	24th		O.O. concerning move of Divs to GHQ area received.	
	25th		OO of 24th cancelled. units ordered to stand fast	
	26th		Preparing to relieve 49th Div, North of 6th Div. CRE & adjt visited CRE 49th Div. Meetings arranged for 27th between O C Fd Coys 14th Div & O C's of Fd Coys of 49th Div whom they expect to relieve.	
	27/28		~~Right~~ Centre sector taken over	
	28/29		Right " "	
	29th		49th RE park & workshops taken over. CRE visited ~~to~~ CRE 49th Divn. CE sixth Corps & took over hutting in Rest area	
	29/30		Left sector taken over. CRE assumed responsibility for all RE work on withdrawal of last of 49th RE	
	~~30th~~ 30		Final conference between CRE's 14th & 49th Div	
	31st		New tramline commenced from Bridge 6 over Y&E Canal.	

FM Close Lt Col
CRE 14th Division
31/12/15

1577 Wt. W10791/1773 500,000 1/15 D. D. & L. A.D.S.S./Forms/C. 2118.

C.R.E.

Please strike off our Nominal Roll

✓ No 89957 Sapper G. Bradford, transferred from this unit to No 4 G.B.D.

~~No 24240 Sapper Foster evacuated sick.~~

Please add to Nominal Roll

2/Lieut Wheeler R.E.

✓ No 62272 S.S. Holt. F.A

21/12/15

C.H.R. Chesney

Captain
~~Major~~, R.E.
Commanding 62nd (Field) Co. R.E.

DAA & QMG, 14 Divn

Forwarded, vide DRO 1029 d/18 12/15.

21 12/15

[illegible]
Lieut & Adjt R.E.
for CRE 14 Divn

Nominal Roll

Headquarters 14th Divisional Engineers

Officers

Lieut Colonel F.M. Close R.E. C.R.E.
Lieut A.R.C. Jenks R.E. (T.C.) - Adjutant.

Captain R. Thomson R.A.M.C. - M.O. i/c 14th Divl Engrs.

Other Ranks.

Regtl No.	Rank & Name	Remarks.
40648	Sergt Major Bayes. D.H. (Class I. W.O.)	
19518	Sergt Owen. A.	
41268	L/Cpl Thornton. W.J.	
48292	Pioneer Smith. R.	
53471	Driver Hogg. A.B.	
61165	" Howe. W.H.	
40127	" Sines. J.	
40934	" Tattersall. J.	
49866	" Wilcock. R.H.	
41383	" Warrington. J.	
46759	Sapper Lane. A.	Attached from 61st Fd Coy R.E. for Supply Wagon.

A.R.C. Jenks
[illegible] Lieut. Col.
C.R.E. 14th Div.

20/12/15.

Nominal Roll
of
Officers, N.C.O.s and Men
of
61st Field Coy Royal Engrs.

[signature]
MAJOR R.E.
COMDG. 61st FIELD Co. R.E.
9.12.15

REGT NO	RANK	NAME	REMARKS.
—	MAJOR	J.P. MACKESY. R.E	
—	LIEUT	E.E.V. TEMPERLEY R.E.(S.R).	
—	"	C.D.A. FENWICK R.E.	
—	"	H.G. ROWLEY. R.E (SR)	
—	"	J.H. WAY-BUCKELL (T.C.) R.E.	
—	II LIEUT	E.A.B. WILLMER R.E.(T.C.)	
40069	CSM	Duley. C.	
40018	Sergt	Watson. S.H.	
40012	"	Hallam. H.	
41866	"	Duckett. W.	
40149	Act/Sergt.	Laverick. A.	
40659	Act/Sergt.	Coyde. S.	
40961	Cpl	Collins. L.	
41020	"	Hands. H.	
41144	"	Lane. J.	
40903	"	Dainty. J.	
40020	"	Parlier. H.	
41910	"	Leonard. J.	
40001	"	Lisle. A.	
41121	"	Roose. F.	

Regt No	Rank	Name	Remarks
40100	II Corpl	Young. F.	
40920	"	Dyer. A.	
45837	"	Little. J.	
40472	"	Clarke. W.	
41851	"	Sharpe. E.	
41875	"	Graham. A.	
42128	"	Ward. A.	
40096		Richards. W.	
41840	Lc Cpl	White. F.	
40191	"	Weston. H.	
40376	"	Campbell. W.	
42122	"	Ankers. E.	
42108	"	Sibley. E.	
49226	"	Batten. W.	
18557	"	Butler. F.	
40148	"	Hillman. F.	
40195	"	Catton. F.	
40962	"	Busby. S.	
40005	"	Bingham. A.	
45078	"	Bradley. H.	

Regt No	Rank	Name	Remarks
40032	C.Q.M.S.	Armstrong. W	
47930	Sergt	Bird. F	
40406		Airey. G.	
41719.	Cpl	Shipton. A.	
40076	II Cpl	Courtney. W.	
41176	L. Cpl	Bailey. A.	
53552		James. D.	
58476		Ham. E.	

Regt. No.	Rank	Name	Remarks
40364	Sapper	Archer. P.	
40646	"	Almond. H.	
41110	"	Armishaw. G.	
42118	"	Armstrong. J.	
40207	"	Ash R.	
49227	"	Alexander. J.	
58352	"	Ashby. W.	
59890	"	Allen. J.	
41687	"	Anthony. W.	
60155	Driver	Ainsworth. W.	
60173	"	Ainger. W.	
61155	"	Atkinson R.	
61147	"	Atkinson. J.	
41073	Sapper	Bees. H	
59385	"	Bennett. C.	
40161	"	Booth. A.	
42362	"	Bolam. J.	
45848	"	Bolton. H.	
36590	"	Bowen. J.	
40194	"	Brown. H.	
40363	"	Brown. F.	
40314	"	Brown. W.	
49235	"	Bradshaw. W.	
40046	"	Brettel. S.	
41786	"	Bruce. J.	
48298	"	Bruce. J.	
40199	"	Burridge. W.	
49655	"	Brum. A.	
40496	Pioneer	Briggs. W.	

Regt No	Rank	Name	Remarks
53553	Dr	Bennett. W.	
40379	Sapper	Campbell. J.	
46894	"	Caulfield. J.	
26510	"	Cassell. G.	
31275	"	Chamberlain. J.	
44916	"	Chamberlain. J.	
40921	"	Childe. C.	
47337	"	Childs. C.	
41164	Pion^r	Cose. A.	
40092	"	Cooper. W.	
34258	Driver	Cameron. W.	
41072	"	Chivers. D.	
40822	"	Cole. S.	
53982	"	Collins. W.	
53983	"	Cotter. J.	
40969	"	Cooks. F.	
44145	"	Crowe. H.	
40274	"	Cropley. H.	
41375	"	Crabbe. F.	
40303	Sapper	Davies. H.	
40142	"	Davies. E.	
40435	"	Doughety. R.	
40025	"	Draper. C.	
61553	"	Dutton. A.	
40433	Pion^r	Dupree. H.	

Regt No.	Rank	Name	Remarks
40707	Driver	Dickinson. J.	
60156	"	Duke. G.	
43558	Sapper	Ellison. F.	
60176	Driver	Emmerson. W.	
40174	Sapper	Fathers. W.	
40354	"	Fadden. M.	
56990	"	Fayackuby. J.	
24854	"	Fellows. E.	
28396	"	Foreman. F.	
49287	"	Fraser. D.	
35935	~~Driver~~ Sapper	Furness. A.	
41123	Driver	Farrer. A.	
33488	Sapper	Gaines. F.	
41126	"	Gallacher. D.	
40742	"	Gallewski. M.	
66306	"	Gay. G.	
34604	"	Gibbs. B.	
10970	"	Gilbert. A.	
41748	"	Gunn. F.	
40255	Pioneer	Gawne. J.	
53984	Driver	Griffiths. J.	

No	Rank	Name	Remarks
40635	Sapper	Wood R.	
55241	"	Wood F.	
46782	Sgt C.S.	Wilkes, H.	
60162	Driver	Wayborn, A.	
40183	"	Walker, R.	
60172	"	Watson, W.	
56738	"	Whitecross, J.	
53988	"	Willcocks, A.	
44511	"	Wills, R.	

Attached by Army on War Establishment

~~M de L C. R. Van Damme Belgian [illegible]~~

No	Rank	Name	Remarks
40492	Sapper	Harker. J.	
36514	"	Harman. G.	
36564	"	Harris W.	
40703	"	Hawkins. W.	
42059	"	Hill. H.	
89891	"	Hoare. J.	
40021	Driver	Hardy. R.	
40432	"	Harris. J.	
44513	"	Hill. S	
40381		Hutchinson. T.	
89009	Sapper	Inder. O	
69516	"	Ingram A.	
40184	Sapper	Jewis. E.	
31064	"	Jolly. J.	
40163	"	Jones. R.	
30918	"	Jones. W.	
45287	Pioneer	Jackson. H.	
41160	D!	Jackson. J.	
89093	Sapper	Kearns. R.	
40737	"	Knight. P.	
41792	Pioneer	Knight. R.	
49865	Driver	King. J.	

No.	Rank	Name	Remarks
40467	Drmr	Slee, J.	
49352	"	Smith, C.	
50730	"	Stier J.	
40721	"	Sunderland, J.	
40140	Sapper	Taylor, J.	
40044	"	Thompson A.	
40484	"	Train J.	
89208		Tray H.	
59393		Turner C.	
41868		Twigger H.	
59422	Sapper	Vaughan F.	
40094	Sapper	Wainwright W.	
43559	"	Wademan W.	
59380	"	Warren H.	
40736	"	Watson R.	
48549	"	Webb, H.	
40874	"	White C.	
48302	"	White O.	
59382	"	Whiteley F.	
40494	"	Willcox C.	
40088	"	Wilson J.	
40437	"	Wilson D.	
33476	"	Witcombe J.	

No	Rank	Name	Remarks
46769	Sapper	Lane. A.	attached H.Q. 14th Div. Engrs.
95049	Sapper	Mara. E.	
40190	"	McConkin. P.	
46715	"	McGinlay. C.	
58968	"	McGowan. H.	
4d2360	"	MaCann. J.	
40186	"	Medhurst. A.	
40401	"	Mitchell. A.	
40108	"	Moore. W.	
95065	"	Mortimer. H.	
49195	"	Mowbray. J.	
40093	"	Mullins. M.	
40413	"	Murphy. D.	
60188	Driver	Martin. G.	
50729	"	McManus. C.	
49215	Sapper	Nesbitt. T.	
47285	"	Nicol. J.	
60151	Driver	Newbury. H.	
34282	"	Northcott. T.	
41065	Sapper	O'Brien. J.	
49587	Driver	O'Neill. R.	

No	Rank	Name	Remarks
56795	Sapper	Partington. J.	
59387	"	Partridge. J.	
40408	"	Pearce. G.	
47120	"	Pearson. A.	
46717		Percival. C.	
40832	Driver	Page. C.	
37806	"	Potter. H.	
53987		Pring. S.	
40603	"	Purslow. W.	
41835	Sapper	Ramsden W.	
59963	"	Reilly. D.	
49624	"	Richardson R.	
42123	"	Riley. E.	
40315	"	Rose. J.	
69195	"	Ryde. A.	
42008	Driver	Rowe. S.	
26680	Sapper	Shaw. A.	
40621	"	Sherry. J.	
40595		Simpson. J.	
40198	"	Skinner. C.	
58166	"	Smith. C.	
26526	"	Smith. G.	
44659		Spray. L.	
45725	"	Stalley. B.	
59678	"	Swatton. A.	
40391	Pioneer	Shrimmin. J.	

Nominal Roll 62nd Fld. Coy R.E.

Officers.

O.C. Captain C. H. R. Chesney R.E.
Captain M. E. Morgan R.E.
Lieut F. M. Jackson R.E.
2/Lieut J. M. Halley R.E.
2/Lieut S. Snell R.E.

NCOs Dismounted No	Rank Name	NCOs Mounted No	Rank Name
44402	S.M. Pearce. F.	47923	2 M.S. Kennedy. T.
40220	Sgt. Pierson J.	58409	F.S. Grant J.
40889	Sgt. Reeves. A.	53599	Cpl. Dawson. H.
41006	" Williams. C.	41413	" Hammond. H.
40181	Cpl. Sharp. J. E.	41251	L/Cpl. Feaver.
41151	" Gill. P.	49873	2/Cpl. Grey. J. C.
41056	" Redfern	60182	L/Cpl. Edwards. J.
41859	" Davey		
40230	" Banks		
40391	" Lawrence		
41105	" Phillips. W. F.		
41161	2/Cpl. MacMasters. A.		
40091	2/Cpl. Roberts. G.		
40197	2/Cpl. King. W. G.		
12297	2/Cpl. Campbell. J.		
40230	2/Cpl. Towell. H.		
40032	" Brewer		
40126	" Armstrong. G.		
48460	" Nevison.		
59305	" Smith. C.		
40234	L/Cpl. Savage. J. W.		
46815	" Dunsire. J.		
40333	" Woods. R. B.		
41083	" Moore. W.		
42035	" Watts. W. J.		
40405	" Robinson. B.		
26963	" Johnstone. A.		
41443	" Tune. A.		
95812	" Forbes. A.		
41796	Sgt. Grice.		

Nominal Roll 62ND Fld Coy R.E.

SAPPERS.

No	Name	No	Name
40047	Sapper Hobley. J.	40706 ~~Sapper~~	Sr Bradshaw J.
40628	" Barber. W.	40271	" Dodds. R.
66312	" Pearce. E.E.	40819	" Edwards. J.
59472	" Rouselle. A.	48141	" Walker A.
45073	" Rochford. J.	41419	" Mc Millan. W.
41200	" Webber. C.	42123	" Paton. D.M.
28296	" Rose. J.	40302	" Storer J.
24755	" Earle E.	40204	" Wilkins
58726	" Thornton W.H.	48723	" Whiteway P.
24412	" Leach W.	40402	" Sutherland
42705	" Massey. W.	42084	" Paine HW.
49351	" Levey.	40165	" Pearce R.C.
40428	" Brooks A.	59448	" Carter R.
40877	" Duncan A.	48922	" Richardson
40918	" Hutton W.	89892	" Ward
40102	" James. A.	40347	" Williams H.L.
41395	" Kelland J.	48897	" Marden J.M.
41884	" Keyse J.B.	48869	" Stewart W.
40058	" Mather A.	33064	" Heath W.
48341	" Medlin	43368	" Cooper. A.
40045	" March. H.W.	61830	" Smith J.
48126	" Smith J.	69957	" Godliman
40118	" Smith. R.G.	95833	" Barrett A.C.
42131	" Smellem. J.	41235	" Bell J.
40111	" Williams J.F.	40938	" Hobbs. F.
49035	" Shannon. H.	48458	" Caley. J.W.
33881	" Moulton W.H.	40705	" Carr. J.
59395	" Sparry	40216	" Gardner. A.
46677	" Begg. J.	40947	" Hanson. H.
33469	" Crawley. W.	41011 ~~[illegible]~~	" Mosley. H.
45623	" Hopkins. J.	40740	" Robson R.W.
22280	" Grant A.	59470	" Dollear A.
49663	" Kriss. H.	48737	" Robertson. A.
34405	" Rickins J.	59386	" Armstrong. M.
95748	" Richards	48895	" Raitt. R.H.
40448	" Knight	49201	" Rodney J.
		63343	" Davison. J.
		44490	" Clements
		~~33159~~	~~" Dillon. E.~~
		26131	" Phillips. G.
		25251	" Morris. F.
		26262	" Coody. J.

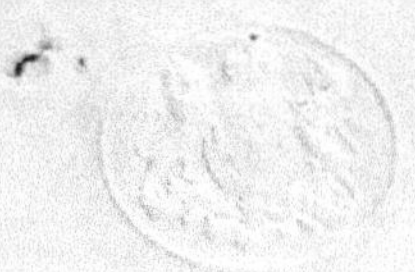

NOMINAL Roll 62ND FLD COY R.E.

SAPPERS contd		PIONEERS	
No	NAME	No	NAME
86899	Sapper Hart	41406	Pioneer Webb A H
69571	" Haslett H	41487	" Holloway J R
69470	" Haslett A	40052	" Oldfield W A
49600	" Houston	40224	" Baulch F H
69955	" Judd H	40106	" Kirkaldy W
95324	" Barr W A	49240	" Watson
40089	" Charles E J	97305	" Woodhouse
40024	" Cockburn W C	41150	" Bonner G
41202	" Eden A	48736	" Mitchell J
40091	" Fletcher G L	40898	" Healey F
40043	" Gentle W	40270	" Pearson
40366	" Hodgson	41214	" Taylor
40068	" Jackson A	40457	" Keane E J
40053	" Lowe A E	63334	" O'Kane W
41394	" Ware J H	40073	" Nason J
40062	" Quinsee C	41514	" Hollingsworth
42340	" Simpson H	59446	" Johnstone
49596	" Whale E	40057	" Bielby A H
40170	" Watts J	48733	" Dick W
40090	" Wilson G J	40097	" Horton S.
41185	" Wilshaw J		
40042	" Webber A		
89214	" Wrigglesworth		
63312	" Childs A		
89695	" Stiley A		
69927	" Burrell J E		
89957	" Bradford G		
69925	" Green A		
33440	" Daly W		
33130	" Creswell J		
59491	" Brown J		

Nominal Roll 62nd Fld Coy R.E.

Mounted

No	Name	No	Name
40684	Driver Bell. R.	49901	Driver McLean
49882	" Bailer. E.	49876	" Lord J.
60185	" Price W.	53993	" Steadman T.
49892	" Munn. W. R.	107475	" Maddams
40754	" Wickenden J. E.	49871	" Watson
49875	" Holt S.	61159	" Brodin
49884	" Isaac J. E.	49864	" Buttle
41399	" Mulligan. S.	49877	" Bentley
49880	" Carman J.	60180	" Jones
61158	" Salmon A. E.	60443	" Inglis
60186	" Reader. J. H.	40765	" Robinson
61150	" Downey J.	49883	" Dowd G.
60184	" Dodds J.		
53900	" Lefley W.		
49881	" McGavin W.		
49867	" Woodgett. H. H.		
60177	" Sawyer T.		
49868	" Hogg W. J.		
40787	" Warburton S.		
53645	" Hazeldene A.		
53992	" Rich A.		
53991	" Musty		
53986	" Livings		
~~53981~~	" Godsave		
49878	" Harrison		
32119	" Fennell		
42852	" Pearse		
40832	" Hills W. R.		
49867	" Wiston. R.		
53558	" Hayward		
61032	" Stingeon		
40663	" Green		
41281	" Clarke. W.		
49872	" Scupham A. G.		
60022	" Martin		

C.H.R. Chesney
Captain ~~Major~~, R.E.
Commanding 62nd (Field) Co. R.E.

NOMINAL ROLL

89TH FIELD CO. R.E.

OFFICERS

CAPTAINS

J. BENSKIN. R.E.
E.O. ALABASTER. R.E.

2ND LIEUTENANTS.

M. C. MOWBRAY. R.E.
T. W. M. BEASLEY. R.E.T.C.
A.W. COOPER. R.E.T.C.
E. D. ALEXANDER. R.E.T.C.

C. S. M. 2ND CLASS W.O
52852. E. LOCKWOOD. R.E.

REG. NO.	RANK AND NAME.	REMARKS.
	SERGEANTS.	
52984	SERGT SHEARMAN. G.	
46282	" MATTHEWS. C.E.	
49000	" ELTON. P.M.	
	CORPORALS	
45196	CORPL KEITH. J.	
45225	" HENLEY. T.	
45169	" HENDRY. R.	
50614	A/ " DUNN. T.	
45223	A/ " BOND. B.	

89th Field. Co. R.E.

Reg. No.	Rank and Name.	Remarks.
	Corporals. Contd.	
45184	A/ Corpl. Muir. E.	
63218	" " Long. H.W.	
49285	" " Mc. Donald. J.	
	2nd Corporals.	
47305	2nd Corpl. Hind. C.	
48525	" " Boyson. J.	
45460	" " Bryce. W.	
49394	A/ " " Shaw. C.	
45181	" " " Searston. C.	
41016	" " " Gray. T.	
45458	" " " White. J.	
40063	2nd Corpl. White. F.	
47296	A/ " " Harman. J. B.	
	Lance Corporals.	
63221	L. Cpl. Shirley. C.	
48519	" " Adams. R.E.	
48430	" " Channing. F.	
63233	" " Midworth. R.	
63219	" " Williams. J.	
45808	" " Grierson. W.	
89907	" " Bransgrove. S.	
89073	" " Millar. S.	
56536	" " King. H.	
65328	" " Stent. G.	

89th FIELD. Co. R. E.

REG. No.	RANK AND NAME.	REMARKS.
	SAPPERS.	
47294	SAPPER ALLAN. A.	
49388	" ARNOLD. A.	
46889	" ABBOTT. J.	
45179	" ACKRILL. H. C.	
63252	" ANGELO. S.	
61521	" ANDREWS. T.	
48894	" ALCOCK. A.	
63217	" ATTENBORROW. T.	
48005	" BAILEY. H. W.	
48541	" BROOMFIELD. W.	
57296	" BROOKS. T.	
61861	" BRANDEN. J.	
49419	" BROOKER. A.	
48534	" BROOKER. H.	
41285	" BABB. W.	
48538	" BROOM. E.	
45449	" BOWNESS. W.	
45187	" BATES. J.	
46912	" BOURNE. L.	
50613	" BOWEN. J.	
48532	" BOYENS. S.	
48509	" BURGOYNE. J.	
45221	" BRIGHT. G.	
45166	" BURNS. T.	
58690	" BALFOUR. S.	
56973	" BUCK. J.	
95834	" BECKETT. W. E.	
45164	" COWAN. D.	
48096	" CHAPMAN. W.	
48097	" CHAPMAN. P.	
45441	" CROPP. E.	
22492	" CLARKE. W. H.	

89th Field. Co. R. E.

Reg. No.	Rank and Name.	Remarks.
	Sappers.	
47284	Sapper Carter. D. W.	
58660	" Chubb. W. R.	
40319	" Dunlop. J.	
45148	" Dunn. H.	
48574	" Dodd. J.	
47780	" Dickens. W.	
48537	" Elleston. F.	
62042	" Edwards. A.G.	
19473	" Evans. J.	
51269	" Fisher. J.	
48513	" Forster. A.	
46891	" Forrester. J.	
48526	" Gibson. G.	
48507	" Garnish. P. B.	
45811	" Grundy. A.	
45186	" Gainey. T.	
48725	" Galloway. A.	
49384	" Gurnett. H.	
47381	" Garrity. D.	
24696	" Garratt. F.	
30463	" Gerrett. L.	
95858	" Golby. G. A.	
49011	" Harris. H. J.	
22081	" Hart. P.	
58828	" Hopkins. W.	
46904	" Hackett. A.	
63234	" Hill. J. H.	
36532	" Hill. J.	
47299	" Holland. W.	
44267	" Holland. W. J.	
42723	" Hobster. E.	
46275	" Horton. S. H.	

89TH FIELD. CO. R.E.

REG. NO.	RANK AND NAME		REMARKS
22986	SAPPER	HAINES. H. J.	
45227	"	HAYNES. G.	
45153	"	HARVEY. A.	
45168	"	HEWSON. T.	
45154	"	HAMILTON. R.	
48515	"	HAYMAN. A.	
89901	"	JONES. J.	
59406	"	KANE. G.	
61809	"	KETLEY. F.	
45144	"	LONGDON. W.	
56604	"	LOOSEMORE. E.	
35877	"	LONG. A.	
63427	"	LYNN. M.	
13970	"	MOORE. E.	
46913	"	MC KENNA. H.	
45807	"	MEALING. T.	
46277	"	MOONEY. E.	
62057	"	MORRIS. B.	
56590	"	MATTHEWS. C.F.	
49403	"	MILNE. R.	
63220	"	MILLS. E. J.	
45446	"	MC KINLEY. T.	
95855	"	MARLOWE. R.	
36046	"	NEWMAN. H.	
45512	"	ORGAN. E.	
48522	"	PLOWMAN. E.	
56975	"	PETTIE. A.	
45228	"	PERCIVAL. B.	
97515	"	PRIOR. B.	
45145	"	READ. J.W.	
45451	"	READSHAW. F.S.	
22166	"	ROGERS. W.	
10275	"	RYMAN. A.	

89TH FIELD. CO. R. E.

REG. NO.	RANK AND NAME	REMARKS.
	SAPPERS CONT.	
48536	SAPPER SCALES. F.	
48523	" SWEPSON. H.	
45806	" STEVENSON. W.	
45191	" SLAUGHTER. J.	
45146	" STOCKTON. T.	
48533	" SCOGING. G.	
48520	" SAUNDERS. W.	
63462	" SOANES. G.	
22856	" SULLIVAN. W.	
48517	" SIMS. F.	
65842	" SHARWOOD. G.	
49205	" STRACHAN. H.	
61599	" TOWNSEND. H.	
45142	" TINKER. E.	
46898	" TOMLINSON. E.	
45226	" WAKELY. E.	
62263	" WEBB. H. W.	
45459	" WEBSTER. J.	
46885	" WILLIAMS. W.	
59377	" WEST. V.	
57367	" WHEELER. J.	
45447	" WATT. L.	
59021	" WOOLLARD. A.	
24602	" CHRISTIAN. M.	

89th Field. Co. R.E.

Reg. No.	Rank and Name.	Remarks.
	Pioneers.	
45161	Pioneer Anderson. J.	
45160	" Bissett. R.	
49206	" Carr. L.	
67847	" Couzens. F.	
46902	" Dick. R.	
45158	" Deacon. A.	
48530	" Foster. E.	
46251	" Jameson. W.	
51677	" Jones. W. E.	
49183	" Kendall. R.	
49236	" Neil. C.	
45156	" Rankin. J.	
31091	" Smith. J.	
36648	" Vickars. W.	
45157	" Whittaker. D.	
45452	" Walker. S.	
48007	" Yarwood. C.B.	
	R. A. M. C.	
36212.	Pte. Brown. J. S.	
11055	" Smith. H.	

89TH FIELD. CO. R.E.

MOUNTED.

REG. NO.	RANK AND NAME.	REMARKS.
	C. Q. M. S.	
48508	A/ SERGT. BELDING. J.	
	FARRIER. SERGT.	
57138	F. SERGT. MORROW. C.	
	SERGEANT.	
53457	SERGT. PETERS. J.	
	2ND CORPORALS.	
58316.	2ND CORPL. HEATH. J.	
53451	A/ " " SIMS. J.	
	LANCE CORPORALS.	
53480	L. CORPL. ANSELL. T.	
61173	" " WARD. C.	
61183	" " HOPE. J.	
	S AND. C. S.	
45448.	S AND. C.S. SHORE. E.	
	DRIVERS.	
53482	DRIVER ALLAN. J.	
53126	" BROWN. J.	
61171	" CRAIG. J.	
61160	" CARRIDICE. W.	
61170	" CARE. W.	
61162.	" COURT.	
53029	" DAVENPORT. A.E.	
53501	" DORWARD. M.	
38310	" DAVEY. W.	
53541	" DUNCAN. A.	

89th FIELD. Co. R.E.

REG. No.	RANK AND NAME.		REMARKS.
53724	DRIVER	EDWARDS. J.	
53461	"	FEARNLEY. W.	
61196	"	HUSH. D.	
53495	"	JACKSON. A.	
61195	"	KING. F.	
52757	"	LEATHERDALE. J.	
53460	"	LEA. W.	
61200	"	MOWAT. J.	
53740	"	MOULDING. W.	
61194	"	McKENZIE. G.	
32554	"	POOLEY. S. A.	
41273	"	PATTERSON. J.	
61164	"	PIKE. E.	
18179	"	PRESTON. J.	
34291	"	PUTTOCK. R.	
61189	"	RALPH. F.	
61186	"	SALMON. J.	
61177	"	SUMNER. W.	
32167	"	SMITH. G. H.	
34362	"	SMITH. W.	
53448	"	SLYFIELD. J.	
34365	"	STRANG. R.	
53453	"	SIMISTER. C.	
61176	"	TOMPSON. G.	
53447	"	THOMPSON. J.	
53469	"	TAYLOR. R.	
53732	"	TULLY. H.	
61161	"	TILLOTSON. I.	
53459	"	TROTT. F.	
34674	"	WEBSTER. G.W.	
53485	"	WILLIAMS. J.	
53470	"	WILLIAMS. W.	
53446	"	WISE. R.	

NOMINAL ROLL OF 14TH SIGNAL COMPANY.

No.	Rank	Name
	Major	Barker E. F. W.
	Lieut:	Anderson A. V.
	2nd Lieut:	Anderson L. G.
	Lieut ~~do~~	Douglas A. H.
	2nd do	Wallace J. C.
	do	Kay C. M.
73579	Corpl (M.C.)	Singer A.
73581	" "	Singer H. A.
32626	Spr	McDonald W.
56436	do	O'Regan P. J.
142313	do	Westbury H. J.
75889	do	Ramsay R.
75720	do	Prendergast J.
72841	Pio.	Peachey F. W.
96639	Spr	Inns F. H.
58747	do	Griffiths A
49411	do	Campion W.
94322	do	Hayward W.
47869	do	Watkins E.
78960	do	Spencers J. V.
42090	Pr.	Copp A. G.
38204	Dr.	Haroard T.
38506	do	Horney J.
38422	do	Dowling J.
37717	do	Gibbons J. F.
50507	do	Parslow J. A.

47957	C.S.M.	Pearks G.S.
47975	C.Q.M.S.	MacIntyre J.
40038	Sergt.	Matthews J.W.
56716	do	Poyser G.L.
56144	a/Sergt	Taylor J.
41827	Corpl	Yates H.A.S.
45057	do	Ross A.
56715	do	Robinson S.E.
56141	a/2/cpl	Phillips B.S.V.
42880	Spr	Thomas C.O.
62135	do	Lake S.
62136	do	Jones J.R.
62129	do	Timson L.H.
62117	do	Griffiths R.
62128	do	Reynolds H.P.
30086	do	Holroyd W.H.
75167	do	McKelland A.E.
40129	do	Gumprecht C.L. alias Marden
44038	Pio.	Collins G.
56321	Spr	Tipton T.N.
41513	do	Mern W.H.
59694	do	Pearce J.
58570	Pio.	Read O.
40639	L/Cpl	Oliver A.
38235	Dr.	Walford W.
60122	do	Anscomb S
60087	do	Barber R.
51379	Spr	Allington R.S.
58737	do	Lynch W.J.
60152	Dr.	Smith S.
47210	Spr	Bailey J.
51375	Dr.	Spencer H.
53209	do	Hancock R.

36176	Spr	Carr N.
56758	do	Haley J.
26723	Pion.	Wilson R
50710	Spr	Smith W.B.
58765	do	Beaumont P.H.
48056	Sergt	Stone R.V.
40115	a/Corpl	Price H.E.J.
47871	L/Cpl	Crutchley P.
58769	L/cpl (unpaid)	Simpson A.
44527	Spr	Tucker C.C.
51377	Dr.	Stone W.J.
40724	Pion.	Gill S.
44040	do	Pearce H.S.
58768	Spr	Templeton J.C.
50749	Dr.	Palmer A.
47870	Pr.	Jones E.
45499	Spr	Dinmouth S.W.
48027	Pion.	Smith W.J.
46772	do	Roseburgh H.M.
51376	Dr.	Christie P.
58764	Spr	Broxholme W.
60134	Dr.	Roberts J.
107354	Spr	Holt W.
56800	do	Hill F
58170	do	James E.
10271	Pte	Delaney J. (1st Dublin Fusiliers)
96508	Spr	Calliley M.
60145	Pion.	Burnham S.W.
37049	Spr	Ketteringham F.J.
60148	Pr.	Taylor P.
56730	a/Corpl	Fowler J.J.
M2/081798	Pte	McDonough M.J. (M.T.A.S.C. attached)
M2/081298	do	Keen W.A. do do

[illegible] Major
Commanding 14th Divisional Signal Coy. R.E.

48045	Pion.	Lane H.C.
40136	L/Cpl	Hunter W.
40069	Spr	Fairclough W.E.
40072	Pion.	Harris J
42589		Williams D.
52370	D.	Bedding J
54019	Sergt (M.C)	Pybus E.
54010	Art. Cpl (MC)	Morgan E.L.
54106	do do	Dolman W.N.
54011	Corpl (MC)	Brand H.G.
59695	do	Parry J
54020	do	Wait R.J.
54105	do	Burton R.B.
41326	do	Geddes W.J.
54276	do	Willis F.C.
40244	do	Webb J.A.
40064	do	Adams H.
40453	do	Hoad J.O.S.
54110	do	Jayes W.
41968	do	Robson J.
54430	do	Fee J.
75666	do	Whittaker E.H.
58741	Sergt	Lester L.E.
42811	a/L/Cpl	Hardwick W.J.
107358	Spr	Wesson W
58767	do	Conway C.
56142	do	Clayton W.J.
51374	D.	Oscroft G.
52335	do	Rennie J.
52817	do	Lumsden J.
112100	do	Applegate M.
60066	do	Tong A.
40079	Spr	Lemon J.

14339	Spr	Peel R.
658	do	Johnson M.
47874	do	White J
48014	do	Rodger W. J.
40483	do	Lewis L.N.
60141	Dr	Green J
52367	Corpl	Greenwood J
48068	L/Cpl	Craig, H.
58887	Spr	Tugwell E.E.
58744	do	Aspden J
62127	do	Green R.J.
56962	do	Keith G.
62130	do	Leeming R.W.J.
53039	do	Wood J.
52341	Dr	Boyle J.
50748	do	Mangan R
60124	do	Hawkes J
60135	do	Watkins R
58774	Spr	Reeves H
47875	do	Francis A.G.
41982	do	Read R
52315	do	Nicholson J.
52372	Corpl	Leaver C.D.
53037	Spr	Moir J.D.
56717	do	Parry E.K.
62134	do	Heppell J.R.
43963	do	Pearson W.H.
40209	L/Cpl	Harris C.
51129	Spr	Cork J
40055	Pion	Hamilton J.
46612	do	Poolman W.G.
60020	Dr	Stevens E.G.
60019	do	Etherden B.

52342 Dr. Nicholson J.
60136 do Ruby F.
621522 Spr Tomsett H.
40894 Sergt. Humm L.A.
43327 Spr Hibbert B.J.
41969 do Grimsey F.
56695 do Brooks A.J.
56958 do Brett A.P.
56696 do Banks L.G.
56677 do Perry H.C.
60149 Dr. Churchward W.
60125 do Pile C.J.
52818 do Ball J.
60143 do Leadbetter A.
24341 do O'Connor P.
48055 L/Cpl Earl H.P.
58751 Pio: Crocker A
60142 Dr. Hutton J.
47986 Sergt Swinney J.
48044 do Thompson R.
48069 a/2/Cpl Dickenson R.
56833 L/Cpl MacIntyre W.S.
40218 do Coe G.H.
44528 Spr Harding F
47878 Pio: Parker H.C.F.
48070 do Lydiate F
51364 Dr. McGongan F
48048 Pio: Ramsay C.
52814 Dr. Cassidy F
40004 ~~48048~~ Spr. Sutton L.
40033 do McCay C
42107 Pio: Cotterill C.
46473 Spr Hipwell W.J.

48052	Spr	Vallens R.
48047	do	Moss E.
26224	Pio[r]	Wilson A. J.
86857	Spr	Eddy C. J.
58743	do	Ritchie M. H.
47478	do	Hastie J. M.
58803	do	Barrie W. M.
22735	do	Reece J.
23526	Pio[r]	Earl G. W.
40497	D[o]	Hember E. P.
60137	do	Taylor A.
80878	do	Dale R.
47842	Sergt	Sharp L.
48227	a/Sergt	Iles E. C.
40645	2/Cpl	Sweeney J.
49586	do	Whittaker A.
42350	L/Cpl	Jones E. R.
41530	Pio[r]	Thorne J.
42089	do	Birch W. W.
58789	Spr	Orchard H.
48076	do	Dale A.
40725	Pio[r]	Hogben W.
60146	D[o]	Baldry W. E.
42043	Pio[r]	Warnes E. R.
51368	D[o]	Wood R.
45137	Pio[r]	Dixon A.
43333	Spr	Reid J.
59805	do	Dunlop T. J.
30816	Pio[r]	Barnett G.
48019	do	Hepburn A.
72852	do	Witham N.
74938	do	Griffiths J. S.
74929	do	Allen J.

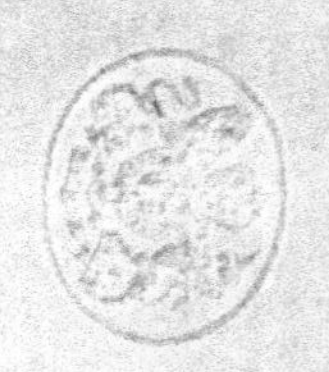

CRE. 14th Div:
Vol: 4

XIV

Confidential

War Diary

of

C.R.E. 14th Divn

from 1-1-16 to 31-1-16

Instructions regarding War Diaries and Intelligence Summaries are contained in F. S. Regs., Part II. and the Staff Manual respectively. Title pages will be prepared in manuscript.

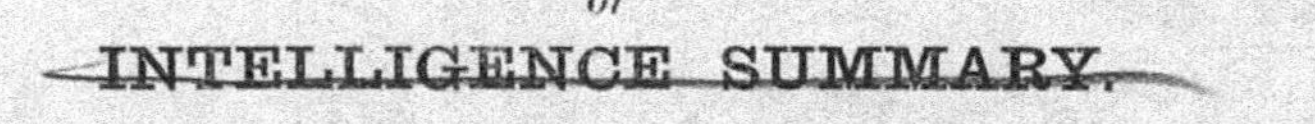

WAR DIARY
or
~~INTELLIGENCE SUMMARY.~~
(Erase heading not required.)

Army Form C. 2118.

Place	Date	Hour	Summary of Events and Information	Remarks and references to Appendices
January	1		Following is present organization of RE.	
61st Co.			Centre sector. 1½ sections at disposal of centre Brigade making breastworks work - Bridges maintenance of Trenches, erecting French dugouts &c, &	
~~62nd Co~~			~~Left~~, 1 Section on hutting, under C.RE., 1 section at disposal of O.C. Coy.	
62nd Co			Left Sector. 1½ sections at disposal of Brigadier Work. ~~Maintenance~~ Maintenance of Bridges, trenches, Erection of French dugouts, & breastworks for support lines 1½ Sections on hutting under C.RE. Other section at disposal of O.C. Coy.	
89th Coy.			~~Left~~ Right Sector. 2 sections at disposal of Brigadier. Work. Maintenance of Bridges & trenches. Breastworks for support line, French dugouts on canal bank, additional trolley line ½ section hutting under C.E. sixth Corps. 1½ sections at disposal of OC.	
Pioneers			1 Coy to each Bde, on communication trenches. 1 ~~pro~~ party responsible for trolley lines. 20 men on hutting. &c.	
	6th		2nd Lt. J.M. Prescott joined 62 Fd Co	

1577 Wt. W10791/1773 500,000 1/15 D. D. & L. A.D.S.S./Forms/C. 2118.

Instructions regarding War Diaries and Intelligence Summaries are contained in F. S. Regs., Part II. and the Staff Manual respectively. Title pages will be prepared in manuscript.

WAR DIARY
or
~~INTELLIGENCE SUMMARY.~~
(Erase heading not required.)

Army Form C. 2118.

Place	Date	Hour	Summary of Events and Information	Remarks and references to Appendices
	Week ending 7th.		Chiefly repair of trenches, erection of French Dugouts &c. Hutting commenced with 2 sections RE, one from 61st Coy & one from 62nd Coy. 61st & 89th Coy extending light railways & laying planks on ~~tram~~ rails for ration parties.	
			1 Coy Pioneers attached 41st Bde employed on erecting French dugouts; extra labour also provided for 42nd Bde. 43rd Bde attaches permanent party to OC 89th Fd Coy.	
	9/10 & 10/11		Line extended to right.	
	7th - 14th.		9th Engineer stores sent up by Rail, & towed by horse along BOESINGHE line. successful. Considerable time wasted through having to bend rails for trench tramways instead of them being sent up as curves. Still, plenty of straight rails.	
			Roll of carpenters in Infantry regiments called for with a view to their employment on hutting as infantry working parties which continually change are useless. This was done before.	
			Repair & screening of canal bridges. &c	
		13th	LANCASHIRE FARM TRAMWAY completed	
	9th		2nd Lt Prescott 62 Fd Co proceeded on sick leave. Leave extended later to 6/2/16 by W.O Authority	

Instructions regarding War Diaries and Intelligence Summaries are contained in F. S. Regs., Part II. and the Staff Manual respectively. Title pages will be prepared in manuscript.

WAR DIARY
or
~~INTELLIGENCE SUMMARY.~~
(Erase heading not required.)

Army Form C. 2118.

Place	Date	Hour	Summary of Events and Information	Remarks and references to Appendices
	10th – 19th		CRE on leave. Major Mackesy acting CRE	
	14th – 23rd		Lieut Jenks Adjt RE to England for investiture (M.C) and then on leave Lieut. JHW Buckell acting adjt	
	18th		2nd Lt. T.W.M. Beasley to England 18/1/16 & report to W.O. Authority A.G. D/1168 & 12/1/16	
	20th		2nd Lt E.A.B. Willmer 61st Co and Lieut 4.M. Jackson 62nd Co evacuated sick	
			CRE visited Canal Bank daily during month except when visiting back area work.	
	23rd		CRE perambulated C. Line in right sector 28.C.20.b & 21a	
	28th		CRE & GSO, perambulated X line from 28 C 27.a.2½7 to C 13.c.5.8	
	29th		CRE visited TROIS TOURS & CANAL BANK centre & left Sectors	
			The principal work in hand during the month has been in front line:–	
			RIGHT SECTOR – recovery of trenches B16 – S+6B – X10., parts of VICAR'S LANE & CLIFFORD'S TOWER	
			Drainage of D21 & THE WILLOWS	
			Erection of Dug outs (French Steel Sectors) on CANAL BANK	
			New Trench Tramway laid from MARENGO HOUSE to AUSTERLITZ FARM	

1577 Wt. W10791/1773 500,000 1/15 D. D. & L. A.D.S.S./Forms/C. 2118.

Instructions regarding War Diaries and Intelligence Summaries are contained in F. S. Regs., Part II. and the Staff Manual respectively. Title pages will be prepared in manuscript.

WAR DIARY
or
~~INTELLIGENCE SUMMARY.~~
(Erase heading not required.)

Army Form C. 2118.

Place	Date	Hour	Summary of Events and Information	Remarks and references to Appendices
			Installation of Electric Light on Canal Bank 28 C 25 a. 5.7	
			Centre Sector - -	
			Wiring in front of C Line + continuation of work on Machineworks C_{10} C_{11} C_{12}	
			Draining D22 — 28.C. 14.d.	
			Erecting dugouts on Canal Bank	
			Laying new trench tramway from BARD COTTAGE to MARENGO HOUSE	
			Repairing LANCASHIRE FARM tram line, + extending it to C 20.a.7.6	
			Left Sector Reclaiming trenches F_{33} F_{34} — 28 C.14 c Very good work done	
			Erecting dugouts on Canal Bank	
			Draining WELLGATE	
			Repairing Bridges	
			Completion of C Line works C_{22} C_{23} + working on C_{18}	
			In addition to above RE work much progress was made in necessary Communication trenches by the 11th Bn King's (LIVERPOOL) Regt (PIONEERS), and M.G. Emplacements + dugouts were constructed by the PIONEER detachment (late Divl Mining Section)	
			Back Area work:- Principally on roads, erection of new Divl H.Q. Huts +	

Instructions regarding War Diaries and Intelligence Summaries are contained in F. S. Regs., Part II. and the Staff Manual respectively. Title pages will be prepared in manuscript.

WAR DIARY
or
~~INTELLIGENCE SUMMARY.~~
(Erase heading not required.)

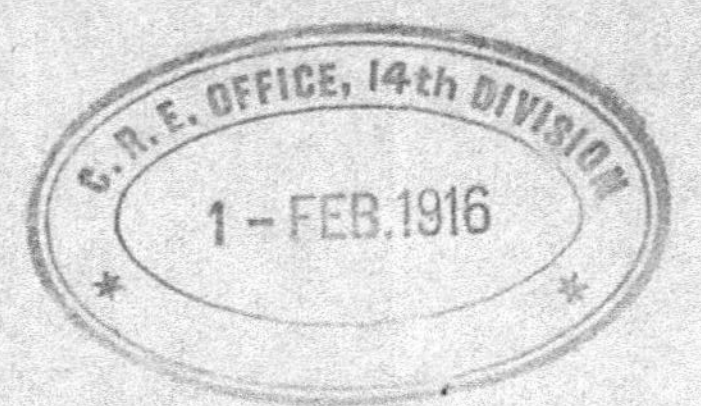

Army Form C. 2118.

Place	Date	Hour	Summary of Events and Information	Remarks and references to Appendices
			work on Divl Rest camps 1.2.3.4 in 28.A also new RE HdQ Huts, and the improvement of 49th Div. Fd. Co Camps (in same map reference)	
	30th		CRE visited BRIELEN	
	31st		CRE visited new camps, workshops etc with Chief Engineer + CRE 20th Div	
			No 97515 Sapper B PRIOR. 89th Field Co RE awarded D.C.M.	
			J M Close Lt Col 1/2/16 CRE 14th Div	

1577 Wt. W10791/1773 500,000 1/15 D. D. & L. A.D.S.S./Forms/C. 2118.

C.R.E. 14th Div:

Vol: 5

Confidential

War Diary
of
C.R.E. 14th Division
from 1st Feby to 29th Feby 16

Instructions regarding War Diaries and Intelligence Summaries are contained in F. S. Regs., Part II. and the Staff Manual respectively. Title pages will be prepared in manuscript.

WAR DIARY
or
~~INTELLIGENCE SUMMARY.~~
(Erase heading not required.)

Army Form C. 2118.

Place	Date	Hour	Summary of Events and Information	Remarks and references to Appendices
	1st Feb 1916		CRE visited X line from Bridge 6X to Wagon Farm, also perambulated C line from C23 to C10	
	3rd		CRE visited L2, Canal bank & FARGATE	Officers of 20th Div visiting line, preparatory to relief
	4th		CRE visited new camp in course of construction.	
	5th		CRE visited BOAR LANE, DAWSON CITY, & Bluffs C8 C7	
	6th		CRE visited P works with GOC XIV Corps & GOC 14 Div.	
	7.		CRE showed party of Canadian Inf. Officers round Instructional School & Workshops	
	9		Visited Canal bank with CRE 20th Div preparatory to handing over.	
	12-13		Division in Corps Reserve – RE HQ to ESQUELBEC	
	17		CRE to FLESSELLES in advance to reconnoitre new area	
	21st		Division to 3rd Army Area. RE HQ at FLESSELLES	
	24th		Division moved North to new area – RE HQ to DOULLENS	
	25th		RE HQ to SUS-ST-LEGER, CRE visited French Div HQ with GOC at BIENVILLE	
	29th		RE HQ to ~~DAINVILLE~~ BARLY. During 25-29 CRE was visiting line & taking over from Corps du Genie. Line in fair condition. Dugouts made by French some 12' deep in chalk are good	

J M Close Lt Col
CRE 14 Div

1577 Wt. W10791/1773 500,000 1/15 D. D. & L. A.D.S.S./Forms/C. 2118.

C.R.E.
14 Div
Vol 6

Confidential

War Diary
of
C.R.E. 14th Division
from 1st March 16 to 31st March 16

Instructions regarding War Diaries and Intelligence Summaries are contained in F. S. Regs., Part II. and the Staff Manual respectively. Title pages will be prepared in manuscript.

WAR DIARY
or
~~INTELLIGENCE SUMMARY.~~
(Erase heading not required.)

Army Form C. 2118.

1.

Place	Date	Hour	Summary of Events and Information	Remarks and references to Appendices
DAINVILLE	1st March.		RE. HQ from BARLY to DAINVILLE : Division front extends from BOYAU 1a & Pt CHATEAU on South to BLANGY ~~inclusive~~ & the River SCARPE on the north. length about 9 kilometres.	
			61st & 59th Fd Cos at disposal of Brigadiers 41st & 43rd Inf Bdes. the Division having two Bdes in line	
	5.		CRE visited BLANGY front line with GSO1, - desirability of early decision as to support line in this quarter pointed out	
			Div front re-organized into 3 Bde Sectors [Right 43 - 42 - 41 Left] 62nd Fd Co at disposal of B.G. 42nd Bde. R.E. companies to have two sections each on front line work. Other sections for improving RE billets in DAINVILLE. French revetting mainly hurdles, satisfactory in this soil	
	6.7.8		CRE perambulated B1 line [LIGNE DE DOUBLEMENT] with GSO1.	
			A small amount of back area improvement work in hand, but materials for both front & back work is still very short	
			Arranged with 185 T. Co RE for training of more mine listeners.	
	8th to 31st.		The principle R.E. work in this sector is the completion of deep mined dugouts	

1577 Wt. W10791/1773 500,000 1/15 D. D. & L. A.D.S.S./Forms/C. 2118.

Instructions regarding War Diaries and Intelligence Summaries are contained in F. S. Regs., Part II. and the Staff Manual respectively. Title pages will be prepared in manuscript.

WAR DIARY

or

~~INTELLIGENCE SUMMARY.~~

(*Erase heading not required.*)

Army Form C. 2118.

3

Place	Date	Hour	Summary of Events and Information	Remarks and references to Appendices
			left incomplete by the French, & the provision of similar ones in the 'B' line or 'Ligne de Doublement'; together with the erection of ferro concrete M.G. Emplacements & Observation posts. French trenches are very inadequately traversed but very well sited; the wiring, especially of the front line trenches, is exceptionally thick. CRE visited front line daily, inspecting work in hand by the Field Cos & 11th Kings Liverpool Regt. Lieut. Rowley died of cerebral meningitis. Major Mackesy appointed CRE 3rd Div.	
			J M Close Lt Col CRE 14 Div.	

Confidential

War Diary
of
C.R.E. 14th Divn
from 1/4/16 to 30/4/16.

Instructions regarding War Diaries and Intelligence Summaries are contained in F. S. Regs., Part II. and the Staff Manual respectively. Title pages will be prepared in manuscript.

WAR DIARY
or
~~INTELLIGENCE SUMMARY.~~
(Erase heading not required.)

Army Form C. 2118.

Place	Date	Hour	Summary of Events and Information	Remarks and references to Appendices
DAINVILLE	1st April to 30th April.		The principal R.E. work continued to be, as regards front line, M.G. emplacements & mined dugouts. In the villages of AGNY & ACHICOURT & in the faubourgs of RONVILLE, ST. SAUVEUR & BLANGY thorough water reconnaisances were carried out & wells recovered & put in good order with a view to increasing the number of points from which water would be obtainable after a bombardment. A scheme for laying on water by pipes to part of the trench system was approved by the Corps., the necessary preliminary levelling done & the stores demanded from Chief Engineer VI Corps.	
			In the billetting area accommodation for officers & men was improved, and a start made at double bunking all available buildings, one section from each Field Co. being so employed.; bunks for 1200 men were completed between the 16th & 30th of April. Improvements to water supply carried out	
			Capt. Benskin R.E. employed at Divisional Instructional School	
			The 11th Kings Liverpools (Pioneer Batn) employed as follows – 1 company with each Brigade & one on the defence of ARRAS.	
			J M Closey Lt Col CRE 14 Div 30/4/16	

Confidential

D.A.G.

[illegible]

[illegible]

[illegible]

[illegible]

2/1/10

[illegible]

Instructions regarding War Diaries and Intelligence Summaries are contained in F. S. Regs., Part II. and the Staff Manual respectively. Title pages will be prepared in manuscript.

WAR DIARY
or
~~INTELLIGENCE SUMMARY.~~
(Erase heading not required.)

CRE 14th Div
May 1916

Army Form C. 2118.

Vol 8

Place	Date	Hour	Summary of Events and Information	Remarks and references to Appendices
DAINVILLE	1st May		CRE on leave until 6th inst. Capt E.F.W. Lees (OC 61st Co RE) acting as CRE. – On the 4th/5th the 41st Inf Bde was taken out of the line, & the left sector previously held by them taken over by the 5th Division. The 61st F.d Co. came out of front line & employed on bunking in WANQUETIN & DAINVILLE.	
	1st–15th May		~~61st Coy training, being inoculated & also some back area work.~~ Field Coys in the line employed on machine-gun emplacements, dugouts & general trench work. Adjt proceeding on leave	
	15th May		Lt Col CLOSE, CRE evacuated sick. Capt C.H.R. CHESNEY OC 62nd Coy acting CRE	
	17th		41st Inf Bde having ~~handed~~ been relieved by a Brigade of 5th Div in the sector immediately south of R SCARPE, the 61st Coy RE who worked in that sector proceeded to WANQUETIN for training. It was desired to send the Coy further back for pontooning practice, but this was not permitted. During training, bombing, musketry, bridging, drill, riding drill was practised. 2/Lt Foster joined 61st Coy RE ~~[illegible]~~ on 1.5.16	
	20th		Capt Lees OC 61st Coy having returned from leave becomes a/CRE.	

1577 Wt. W10791/1773 500,000 1/15 D. D. & L. A.D.S.S./Forms/C. 2118.

Instructions regarding War Diaries and Intelligence Summaries are contained in F. S. Regs., Part II. and the Staff Manual respectively. Title pages will be prepared in manuscript.

WAR DIARY
or
INTELLIGENCE SUMMARY.
(Erase heading not required.)

CRE 14th Div
May 1916

Army Form C. 2118.

Place	Date	Hour	Summary of Events and Information	Remarks and references to Appendices
Dainville	20th 5/16		Conference held by C E of CRE's of Divisions to consider problem of next winters hutting. A/CRE + Capt Chesney RE attended. 62nd + 89th Coys commence scheme for water supply + storage in that part of the trenches where water has to be carried furthest; the necessary stores having commenced to arrive. It was decided to dig in the pipe line, which was 6000 yds long, to a depth of 4 ft. This progressed very slowly owing to the lack of working parties. The supply was to be taken from Arras town mains which were still in working order, under charge of a French Officer who had emergency plant stored in a dugout. Work on Arras defences continued by 3 platoons (approx.) of Pioneer Regt. A company of Pioneers which had been working on I sector was employed, on the handing over of that sector, on the defences of the village of ~~Achicourt~~ ACHICOURT, a strong point somewhat behind the chain of existing strong points, which had not hitherto received much attention. The defensive mining on the front was done by a detachment of infantry,	

1577 Wt. W10791/1773 500,000 1/15 D. D. & L. A.D.S.S./Forms/C. 2118.

Instructions regarding War Diaries and Intelligence Summaries are contained in F. S. Regs., Part II. and the Staff Manual respectively. Title pages will be prepared in manuscript.

WAR DIARY
or
INTELLIGENCE SUMMARY.
(Erase heading not required.)

CRE 14th Div

May 1916.

Army Form C. 2118.

Place	Date	Hour	Summary of Events and Information	Remarks and references to Appendices
			special men & officers who had previous experience. Later on one section of the New Zealand Engineers Tunnelling Coy was transferred to work at one place where the enemy had pushed forward.	
			J C Rastin [?] Lt Col RE CRE 14th Div	

1577 Wt. W10791/1773 500,000 1/15 D. D. & L. A.D.S.S./Forms/C. 2118.

C.R.E. OFFICE, 14th DIVISION
4 - JUL. 1916

Confidential

DAG

Herewith War Diary of CRE 14th Div for June 1916

4/7/16

A H Jenk[illegible]
Lt Col Adjt RE
14th Div.

Instructions regarding War Diaries and Intelligence Summaries are contained in F. S. Regs., Part II. and the Staff Manual respectively. Title pages will be prepared in manuscript.

WAR DIARY
or
~~INTELLIGENCE SUMMARY.~~
(Erase heading not required.)

CRE 14th Div
June 1916

Army Form C. 2118.
June
C.R.E. 14 Div
Vol 9

Place	Date	Hour	Summary of Events and Information	Remarks and references to Appendices
Dainville 1.6.16			Disposition of RE Coys:- 61st Coy Training in rest area 62nd Coy working with 42nd Inf Bde in H Sector of front 89th Coy - - - 43rd Inf Bde in G Sector of front. Major E F W Lees O C 61st Coy acting as CRE	
5th & 6th.			61st Coy take over from 89th Coy the work in G Sector, the latter going for rest & training to Wanquetin, practising musketry, drill, bombing &c & ~~[illegible]~~ some RE work.	
14th			Orders received that certain special ~~special~~ work was to be commenced & completed by evening of 18th. One section of 89th Coy brought back to work in the workshops. One company of Pioneers do the necessary digging & carrying done by Infantry.	
night 17/18th			Work completed	
17th			Lt. Col JEECRASTER RE took up duties of CRE	
18th			Orders received to take over ~~H~~ I. J. & K sectors from 5th Div & to hand over G sector to 55th Div. The Div' Front to extend thus from a point opposite Achicourt to North of ROCLINCOURT, ~~round ARRAS~~ ie a line about 12,000 yard long in front of ARRAS	
19th - 22nd			Taking over & handing over in progress. 89th Coy recalled from WANQUETIN to relieve	

1577 Wt. W10791/1773 500,000 1/15 D. D. & L. A.D.S.S./Forms/C. 2118.

Instructions regarding War Diaries and Intelligence Summaries are contained in F. S. Regs., Part II. and the Staff Manual respectively. Title pages will be prepared in manuscript.

WAR DIARY
or
~~INTELLIGENCE SUMMARY.~~
(Erase heading not required.)

CRE 14th Div

June 1916

Army Form C. 2118.

Place	Date	Hour	Summary of Events and Information	Remarks and references to Appendices
			1/2 Durham Fd Coy in K Sector: ~~58th Coy~~ whole Coy billeted in ARRAS with transport in WARLUS. 61st Coy relieve 59th Coy in J Sector & ½ I sector, billeted in ARRAS with transport in WARLUS: 62nd Coy extends to left & takes over other half of J sector. Transport in WARLUS, Coy HQ & 1 Section in DAINVILLE, 3 sections in ARRAS	
23rd-30th			Field Coys employed in making Trench Mortar & M/G emplacements, & assisting Infantry to consolidate the 7 craters in K & J sectors. Work hindered by enemy activity. On 27th a special demonstration carried out against BEAURAINS. During this period practice wire-cutting carried out by ~~enemy~~ British artillery & trench mortars, the gaps in the wire being covered at night by machine guns.	
			Major DUIGAN comdg New Zealand Tunnelling Coy accidentally injured.	
			Note: H Sector extends from M 10 c central to G 35 b 9.1 I " " G 35 b 9.1 northward to R Scarpe J " " R Scarpe to G 6 c central K " " G 6 c central to A 23 c 8.3 } Sheet 51 B.	

J.C. Rastie
Lt Col RE
CRE 14th Div

1577 Wt. W10791/1773 500,000 1/15 D. D. & L. A.D.S.S./Forms/C. 2118.

CONFIDENTIAL.

War Diaries

of

C.R.E.14th Division, 61st, 62nd & 89th Field Companies R.E.,

From 1st July 16 to 31st July 16.

****

Instructions regarding War Diaries and Intelligence Summaries are contained in F. S. Regs., Part II. and the Staff Manual respectively. Title pages will be prepared in manuscript.

WAR DIARY

~~or~~

~~INTELLIGENCE SUMMARY.~~

(Erase heading not required.)

H.Q. 14th Divn R.E.

July 1916

Army Form C. 2118.

Place	Date	Hour	Summary of Events and Information	Remarks and references to Appendices
DAINVILLE	1st	10.45 pm	Enemy fired a mine at 10.45 pm and destroyed front line trench in 113 trench K sector. Crater formed 150' across with an equal lip all round. Crater was immediately occupied by 8th KRRC. A few Germans who attempted to enter it were driven off and front lip was occupied. Warning of this mine had been given some days previously by the 184 Tunnelling Co: R.E. and the front trench had been cleared for 30 yds on each side of what was believed to be the danger point. Stores for consolidating the crater had also been collected in the front line trench. These were buried by the lip of the crater which was larger than anticipated. Total casualties caused by mine explosion and in holding crater 33 Infy.	
	2nd	9.30 am	CRE arranged with O.C. 89th Co R.E. and 41st Infy. Brigade for sending up stores and consolidation of new crater referred to above.	
		9 pm	1 NCO and 8 sappers assisted in consolidation of crater. Work much interfered with by trench mortar bombs. Northern sap leading to crater largely destroyed. Casualties 11 Infy.	
	3rd	10 am	CRE visited new crater with O.C. 89th Co R.E.	
		5 pm	CRE had a conference with Brigade Commander and O.C. 184th Tunnelling Co: R.E. with regard to mining situation in K sector. It was pointed out that the outer lip of the new crater would probably be blown up by the enemy in 10 days time. Also that he might fire a new mine near the junction of 113 and 114 in about 3 days. It was decided to start consolidation of rear lip of crater in 113 and to open out an old trench about 60 yds behind the front line and wire it. Arrangements to be made for consolidation of new crater if formed at junction of 113 and 114. Tunnelling Co: to try to camouflet the enemy's gallery opposite ~~113~~ junction 113 and 114 and to start a new gallery from the bottom of crater in 113. 41st Infy Brigade and 89th Co R.E. informed of these decisions and asked to put work in hand.	

1577 Wt. W10791/1773 500,000 1/15 D. D. & L. A.D.S.S./Forms/C. 2118.

Instructions regarding War Diaries and Intelligence Summaries are contained in F. S. Regs., Part II. and the Staff Manual respectively. Title pages will be prepared in manuscript.

WAR DIARY
or
INTELLIGENCE SUMMARY.
(*Erase heading not required.*)

Army Form C. 2118.

Place	Date	Hour	Summary of Events and Information	Remarks and references to Appendices
Dainville	4.7.16		2/Lt C V SANDEMAN 184th Tunnelling Coy RE killed by shell fire in trenches.	
~~4.7.16~~ 7			Enemy blew small mine close to an existing crater, removing part of lip but doing no other damage	
~~7.7.16~~	7.7.16		One section from 61st Co & one section from 62nd Co attached to 184th Coy for work on ~~crater~~ consolidation of crater blown on 1st inst, the work being considerably interfered with by the enemy trench mortars.	
			CRE went round craters ~~with~~ in K sector with officers of 61st and 62nd Cos. RE afterwards visited battalion H.Q. in ROCLINCOURT	
		8.30pm	DAINVILLE having been constantly shelled during past week H.Q. divl RE were moved to the BRIQUETERIE on the WARLUS - WANQUETIN road	
BRIQUETERIE WARLUS	8.7.16	9.30am	CRE inspected transport of field Cos. at WARLUS	
		5.0pm	CRE had a conference with director of mines 3rd Army. The latter considered that it was useless to try to blow away the forward lip of the new crater in K113 and recommended that work on the gallery in the crater should therefore be stopped	
	9.7.16	9.30am	CRE had conference with Divl Commander C.E. VIth Corps and Controller of Mines 3rd Army with ref: to mining policy. It was decided to open up an old trench behind the front trench at 116a sap in K sector as enemy had been heard working close to the sap and it was probable he would fire a mine at that point	
		10.30am	CRE visited Field Cos. RE in ARRAS.	

1577 Wt. W10791/1773 500,000 1/15 D. D. & L. A.D.S.S./Forms/C. 2118.

Army Form C. 2118.

Instructions regarding War Diaries and Intelligence Summaries are contained in F. S. Regs., Part II. and the Staff Manual respectively. Title pages will be prepared in manuscript.

WAR DIARY
or
INTELLIGENCE SUMMARY.
(Erase heading not required.)

Place	Date	Hour	Summary of Events and Information	Remarks and references to Appendices
BRIQUETERIE WARLUS	10.7.16	10 am	CRE visited Field Cos. RE. in ARRAS. Afterwards visited QUATRE VENTS with OC 89th Field Co. RE. to arrange for building brigade battle HQ. at that point.	
		1 pm	CRE visited New Zealand Engineer Tunnelling Co. to discuss mining situation in J sector.	
		2 pm	CRE visited 43rd Infy. Brigade HQ.	
"	11.7.16		Enemy fired a camouflet north of 113 Crater in K sector. A little chalk was thrown into the crater and about 20ft of gallery in our K10 mine destroyed. The firing of this camouflet by the enemy eases the situation at this point. He has not destroyed 113 crater as it was feared he might. The danger of his firing a mine and destroying our trench at the junction of 113 and 114 is removed for the present.	
		9.30 am	CRE visited ROCLINCOURT and craters in K sector with C.E. VIth Corps and O.C 89th Co. RE. Afterwards visited the water supply to the redoubt line, and examined October Avenue with a view to laying a trench tramway along it from the Candle Works to the support line.	
"	12.7.16	9.30 am	CRE visited 61st Field Co. RE. in ARRAS to arrange for work on the tramway in October Avenue and for burying the water main from St NICHOLAS to the redoubt line. 300 Infy and a section of the 67th Field Co RE. all from the 11th Divn to be lent to 61st Field Co. RE. for this work. Afterwards visited 89th Co RE.	
	13.7.16	9.30 am	CRE visited 61st and 89th Cos. RE. and 41st Brigade.	
	14.7.16	10 am	CRE attended conference at 41st Brigade re: employment of pioneers on 41st and 43rd Brigade sectors. Afterwards visited 61st and 89th Cos. RE.	

1577 Wt. W10791/1773 500,000 1/15 D. D. & L. A.D.S.S./Forms/C. 2118.

Instructions regarding War Diaries and Intelligence Summaries are contained in F. S. Regs., Part II. and the Staff Manual respectively. Title pages will be prepared in manuscript.

WAR DIARY
or
~~INTELLIGENCE~~ SUMMARY.
(Erase heading not required.)

Army Form C. 2118.

14th Divl. RE. July 1916

Place	Date	Hour	Summary of Events and Information	Remarks and references to Appendices
WARLUS BRIQUETERIE	15.7.16	9.30am	CRE visited 89th and 61st Fld Cos RE. Afterwards visited trench tramway work in October avenue and support and front line in J.1. sector.	
		2pm	CRE visited 42nd Brigade.	
	16.7.16	~~9.30~~ 12 noon	CRE visited CRE 46th Divn at BAVINCOURT to see expanded metal mats used for crossing wire entanglements. One specimen brought back.	
	17.7.16	9.30am	CRE visited 61st and 89th Field Cos RE and 41st Infy. Brigade	
	18.7.16	9.30am	CRE went round OILWORKS, FORESTIER, NICHOLLS and BOSKY redoubts with GSO1 and inspected work on trench tramway. Afterwards visited 89th and 61st Cos RE and 41st and 43rd Brigades	
	19.7.16	9.30am	CRE attended conference of Brigadiers re organisation of work and working parties. Afterwards visited 89th and 61st Cos RE	
	20.7.16	9.30am	CRE visited 89th and 61st Cos RE. Company commanders warned to be ready to move on the 31st inst	
	21.7.16	9.30am	CRE visited 89th and 61st Cos RE. Afterwards visited new brigade battle HQ at QUATRE VENTS with OC 89th Co RE	
	22.7.16	9.0am	Arranged handing over of work in H sector to CRE 11th Divn. Visited DAINVILLE workshops with CRE 11th Divn. 62nd Co RE handed over work in H sector to 68th Co RE 11th Divn on night 22/23rd. 62nd Co RE took over work in left of I sector from 61st Co RE	
	23.7.16	9.0am	CRE visited RE transport at WARLUS and inspected wagons. J sector bombarded for 1 hour about 10pm much damage to trenches	
	24.7.16	9.0am	CRE went round redoubt line from FORESTIER redoubt to ROCLINCOURT with CRE 21st Divn preparatory to handing over J and K sectors. One section 62nd Co RE moved to BRIQUETERIE for training	
	25.7.16	9.30am	CRE visited 89th and 61st Cos RE and arranged handing over of J and K sectors to 11th Divn	

1577 Wt. W10791/1773 500,000 1/15 D. D. & L. A.D.S.S./Forms/C. 2118.

Army Form C. 2118.

Instructions regarding War Diaries and Intelligence Summaries are contained in F. S. Regs., Part II. and the Staff Manual respectively. Title pages will be prepared in manuscript.

WAR DIARY
or
~~INTELLIGENCE SUMMARY.~~ 14th Divl RE. H.Q.

(*Erase heading not required.*)

Place	Date	Hour	Summary of Events and Information	Remarks and references to Appendices
BRIQUETERIE near WARLUS	26.7.16	9.0 am	CRE handing over plans etc. of J and K sectors to CRE 21st Div. Work in I sector handed over from 62nd Co. RE to 68th Co. RE (11th Div) on night 26th/27th	
"	27.7.16	9.0 am	CRE handed over I sector to CRE 11th Div. DAINVILLE workshops handed over by 11th Kings Liverpool Regt (Pioneers) to 11th Div	
		6 pm	62nd Co. RE less 1 sect moved from ARRAS and DAINVILLE to BRIQUETERIE	
"	28.7.16	8 am	62nd Co. RE moved from BRIQUETERIE to IVERGNY	
		7 pm	61st Co. RE moved from ARRAS to BRIQUETERIE. Instructions issued to Field Cos. RE re the work of the RE in consolidation of points during an attack.	
"	29.7.16	8 am	61st Co. RE moved from BRIQUETERIE to SUS-ST-LEGER. ~~89th~~ 62nd Co. RE from IVERGNY to BARLY. 89th Co. RE moved from ARRAS to BRIQUETERIE.	
"	30.7.16	8.30 am	H.Q. Divl. RE marched from BRIQUETERIE to SUS-ST-LEGER. 61st Co RE marched to BONNIERE. 62nd Co. RE halted at BARLY. 89th Co RE marched from BRIQUETERIE to SOMBRIN	
SUS-ST-LEGER	31.7.16	8.30 am	H.Q. Divl RE marched from SUS-ST-LEGER to BÉALCOURT. 61st Co. RE halted at BONNIÈRE. 62nd Co. RE marched from BARLY to St HILAIRE. 89th Co RE marched from SOMBRIN to BARLY	
		10.30 am	CRE visited 61st Co. RE at BONNIERE	

1577 Wt. W10791/1773 500,000 1/15 D. D. & L. A.D.S.S./Forms/C. 2118.

SECRET.

Consolidation of Points during an Attack.

The following notes are based on information supplied by the C.R.E. 21st Division with regard to recent operations on the SOMME.

Selection of Points. 1. The points to be consolidated should be selected before the attack and their positions marked on all maps.

Points selected for consolidation should fulfill the following conditions as far as possible

(a) They should not be under direct observation from the enemy's positions.

(b) They should be sited so that they can mutually support each other.

The number of points selected must depend on the labour available. One R.E.Section can construct a point for a garrison of one platoon.

Responsibility for construction. 2. The R.E. are normally responsible for the construction of strong points. The Infantry are responsible for the construction of fire trenches connecting them and for communication trenches.

Allotment of R.E. 3. The Field Companies R.E., detailed for consolidation will usually work under the orders of the C.R.E. and will not be allotted to Infantry Brigades.

Orders to commence work. 4. In order to save time it will generally be convenient if Brigades inform the Field Companies R.E., when the objective has been obtained and consolidation can commence. But it is important that the objective should be firmly held before the R.E. move up. Otherwise they will become involved in the fight, and no work will be done.

Reliefs for R.E. 5. Arrangements must be made for providing reliefs for the R.E., so that work may proceed without interruption. A convenient distribution is to allot two Field Cos R.E., for the first 8 hours relief and one Field Coy R.E., for the second.

Design of Strong Points. 6. Only general instructions can be issued before hand as to the design of strong points. The details of each point must be settled and marked out on the ground by the R.E.Officer Commanding the consolidating party.

Tools and Stores. 7. Every man of the consolidating party will carry with him a load of tools and stores.

Mobile R.E. Park. 8. A Mobile R.E.Park will be formed composed of the 9 pontoon wagons of the Field Companies R.E., and such other wagons as may be available. These wagons will be loaded with wire, pickets, timber, corrugated iron, sandbags, explosives, ammunition and water. A R.E.Officer will be placed in command of the Mobile R.E.Park.

Forward R.E. Dumps. 9. Positions for one or more forward R.E.Dumps will be selected. These will be at the furthest points to which horse transport can proceed. As soon as the objectives are attained the Mobile R.E.Park will move forward and deposit its material at the forward dumps. The O.C. will inform the consolidating parties as soon as a dump has been formed. When the Wagons are unloaded the Mobile R.E.Park will return and load up. Wagons are always to be kept fully loaded with teams ready to hook in.

J.C. Rustin

27th July 16.

Lieut Colonel R.E.,
C.R.E.14th Division.

C O N F I D E N T I A L.

Sept 17

W A R   D I A R Y.

OF

HEADQUARTERS: ROYAL ENGINEERS

14TH (LIGHT) DIVISION.

(Volume)

August 1916

ND

14 / CRE Vol 11

Instructions regarding War Diaries and Intelligence Summaries are contained in F. S. Regs., Part II. and the Staff Manual respectively. Title pages will be prepared in manuscript.

WAR DIARY
or
~~INTELLIGENCE~~ SUMMARY. H.Q. 14th Div'l RE

(*Erase heading not required.*)

Army Form C. 2118.

August 1916

Place	Date	Hour	Summary of Events and Information	Remarks and references to Appendices
BEALCOURT	1.8.16	9.30am	HQ Div'l RE marched to BERNAVILLE. 61st Co. RE marched from BONNIERE to GRIMONT. 62nd Co: RE halted at St HILAIRE. 89th Co: RE marched from BARLY to GEZAINCOURT.	
BERNAVILLE	2.8.16	9.15am	CRE visited 61st, 62nd, and 89th Cos: RE. and gave them instructions as to training etc:	
"	3.8.16		CRE employed in office	
"	4.8.16	10am	CRE visited CRE 7th Div at BELLOY-SUR-SOMME to obtain information re: recent RE work during the SOMME operations	
"	5.8.16	9am	CRE held a conference of field Co: commanders to discuss the work of the RE during an attack	
"	6.8.16	11.30am	Transport of HQ RE and field Cos: RE marched to FLESSELLES area	
"	7.8.16		61st and 89th Cos: RE moved by rail from CANDAS to ~~BERNANCOURT~~ MERICOURT L'ABBE and marched to DERNANCOURT. ~~[illegible]~~ 62nd Co: RE by rail from CANDAS to MERICOURT L'ABBE and marched to BUIRE SUR L'ANCRE. RE transport marched by road to rejoin units at above places. HQ RE by road to BUIRE SUR L'ANCRE	
BUIRE SUR L'ANCRE	8.8.16	2.30pm	CRE visited field Cos: RE. Orders received for 14th Div to take over from 17th Div XV th Corps 4th Army on 12/13 Aug.	2nd Lieut J. RITCHIE RE(TC) joined 62nd Co RE 8/8/16
"	9.8.16	9.30am	CRE visited CRE 17th Div at BELLEVUE FARM to arrange taking over.	
		4pm	CRE visited 62nd Field Co RE.	
"	10.8.16	5.30am	CRE went to HQ 17th Div: afterwards visited the trenches held by the 17th Div between DELVILLE WOOD and SEAFORTH TRENCH including support and communication trenches also Brigade and Bn Headquarters	
		6.30pm	CRE visited Chief Engineer XV th Corps	

1577 Wt. W10791/1773 500,000 1/15 D. D. & L. A.D.S.S./Forms/C. 2118.

Army Form C. 2118.

Instructions regarding War Diaries and Intelligence Summaries are contained in F. S. Regs., Part II. and the Staff Manual respectively. Title pages will be prepared in manuscript.

WAR DIARY
or
INTELLIGENCE SUMMARY.
(Erase heading not required.)

Place	Date	Hour	Summary of Events and Information	Remarks and references to Appendices
BUIRE SUR L'ANCRE	11.8.16	8 am	CRE visited CRE 17th Div to take over plans etc and discuss future work.	
		6 pm	Orders issued to 61st 62nd and 89th Field Cos: RE and 11th Kings Liverpool Regt: Pioneers to take over billets and work from corresponding ~~numbers~~ units of 17th Div on the night 12/13th. Work to start on morning of 13th. Work consists of digging of communication and support trenches and wiring of latter.	
"	12.8.16	9.45 am	CRE visited CRE 17th Div re taking over work. Afterwards visited 61st 62nd and 89th Field Cos: RE and discussed programme of work. RE companies and Pioneers moved to billets of RE & Pioneers of 17th Div. at 4.30 pm	
"	13.8.16	8.15 am	CRE moved to new Divl HQ at BELLE VUE farm.	
		2 pm	CRE visited the Field Cos: RE at their bivouacs S.W. of MAMETZ. Also visited HQ of 41st and 43rd Infy: brigades in POMMIER redoubt. Field companies employed during the day in renovating old German second and support lines west of LONGUEVAL and on communication trenches leading to them.	
BELLEVUE Farm	14.8.16	9.30 am	CRE and adjutant visited CRUCIFIX ALLEY and SAVOY and CARLTON trenches. 61st Co. employed on SAVOY trench, 89th Co. on CARLTON trench each with one Co: Pioneers. 2 Secs 62nd Co. and 1 Co Pioneers employed with 41st Brigade on front trenches in vicinity of PONT STREET and PEAR STREET. Major LEES 61st Co. RE marked out a trench for a support line in continuation of SAVOY trench through DELVILLE WOOD. Capt BENSKIN marked out a continuation of CRUCIFIX ALLEY towards DELVILLE WOOD but was stopped by shell fire. Capt: ALABASTER 89th Co. RE. wounded by shell fire. 1 O.R. killed 4 O.R. wounded.	
"	15.8.16	10 am	CRE visited Field Cos: RE and Pioneers. During the night 14/15 CRUCIFIX ALLEY was extended 460 yds towards DELVILLE WOOD and its continuation through DELVILLE WOOD marked out (89th Co & 300 Infy) New support trench in DELVILLE WOOD commenced (61st Co and 300 Infy) Allotment of work as follows for 16.8.16. SAVOY trench 61st Co and 2 platoons pioneers. CARLTON trench 89th Co and 2 platoons Pioneers. 1 Co Pioneers & 2 Secs 62nd Co RE with 41st Brigade. 1 Co Pioneers with 43rd Brigade	

Army Form C. 2118.

Instructions regarding War Diaries and Intelligence Summaries are contained in F. S. Regs., Part II. and the Staff Manual respectively. Title pages will be prepared in manuscript.

WAR DIARY
or
INTELLIGENCE SUMMARY.
(Erase heading not required.)

Place	Date	Hour	Summary of Events and Information	Remarks and references to Appendices
BELLEVUE FARM	~~23~~ 16.8.16	9.30a	CRE. Attended Divl. conference with ref. to proposed attack on enemy's trenches WOOD LANE, ORCHARD TRENCH, DELVILLE WOOD, and BEER TRENCH. Points for 6 strong points were selected. To be each constructed by 1 Sec. RE and 1 platoon pioneers.	Maps X12a and X12b
		11.45a	CRE held a conference with the Field Co. Commanders and O.C. 11th Kings Liverpool Regt (Pioneers) with ref. to the method of carrying out the above work.	
			Casualties to noon O.R. 1 killed 2 wounded 1 missing. Dump of RE stores formed near site of strong points night 16/17	
"	17.8.16	1.15a	CRE issued operation order No 5 for 18th Aug (Copy attached)	
		9.30a	CRE visited 41st & 43rd Infy: Brigades Field Cos: and 11th Kings Liverpool Regt. with ref. to consolidation of strong points after the attack on the 18th	
"	18.8.16		Bombardment of enemy's positions commenced from 8a.	
		2.45p	Infantry of the division assaulted the enemy's trenches right and left of DELVILLE WOOD. Both attacks gained objective except ~~when~~ between T13.a.0.7. and S18b.7.9. where position still obscure.	
		6.48p	O.C. 61st Co. RE reported digging commenced on MARS work at S.18d 6.5. (South of ~~right~~ east end of DELVILLE WOOD) No work possible as yet on VENUS work (T.13a.0.7.) or SATURN work (S18b.7.9.) Doubtful if any wiring can be done before night. Line from S.18.d.6.4 to junction of HOP ALLEY with BEER TRENCH fairly well dug in by infantry. Communication understood to be through between S18d.6.4. and S18b.0.4. Lieut. BUCKLE wounded.	
			62nd Co. RE constructed and wired strong points at S11c 5.9 and S.11.d.0.8 in front of ORCHARD TRENCH. No work possible on strong point on FLERS road owing to proximity of the enemy in DELVILLE WOOD. 2nd Lieuts MILLEN and WHEELER 62nd Co. RE wounded. Other casualties 61st Co. 7 O.R. wounded 1 O.R. missing. 62nd Co. RE. 1 O.R. killed. 3 O.R. wounded.	
			Lieut. G. WALKER R.E.(T.C.) joined 89th Co. RE	

1577 Wt. W10791/1773 500,000 1/15 D. D. & L. A.D.S.S./Forms/C. 2118.

Army Form C. 2118.

WAR DIARY
or
INTELLIGENCE SUMMARY.
(Erase heading not required.)

Instructions regarding War Diaries and Intelligence Summaries are contained in F. S. Regs., Part II. and the Staff Manual respectively. Title pages will be prepared in manuscript.

Place	Date	Hour	Summary of Events and Information	Remarks and references to Appendices
BELLEVUE FARM	19.8.16	8.30	CRE visited 41st 42nd and 43rd Infy: Brigades, 61st 62nd and 89th Cos RE and 11th Kings Liverpool Regt Pioneers to collect reports as to work done during the attack on the previous day and future requirements.	
"	20.8.16	8.30 am	CRE attended Divl: Conference at POMMIER redoubt to discuss impending operations. Afterwards visited 61st 62nd 89th Cos RE and 11th Kings Liverpool Regt. Pioneers. The following allotment was made To 41st Infy. Brigade 2 Secns 62nd Co. RE and 1 Coy Pioneers for construction of support trenches etc. in DELVILLE WOOD. To 42nd Infy. Brigade 2 Secns 89th Co RE and 1 Coy Pioneers for the same work. 61st Co. RE to construct a new Battalion H.Q. in DELVILLE WOOD, and to extend CRUCIFIX ALLEY to front line with the help of 1 Co: Pioneers. 62nd Co. RE to construct a H.A. O.P. in LONGUEVAL	
"	21.8.16	1.15	Operation order received for an attack to be made by 41st Infy. Brigade on certain points of the INNER trench held by enemy in DELVILLE WOOD. For this operation A.P.C. 41st Infy. Brigade asked for the 62nd Fld Co. RE to assist in consolidating the points after they were taken. This was approved by the Divl: Commander and the company detailed. The whole of the 89th Co. RE was allotted to 42nd Infy Brigade to assist in digging support and communication trenches.	
		5 pm	The attack made by the 41st Infy: Brigade ~~at~~ on INNER TRENCH did not succeed and the 62nd Co: RE were not utilised	
"	22.8.16	9 am	The Field Cos: + Pioneers were reallotted as follows To 41st Infy. Brigade 62nd Co RE and 1 Co: Pioneers to 42nd Infy: Brigade 89th Co RE and 2 Cos. Pioneers. 2 Secns of 61st Co: RE to assist 89th Co RE as required. In reserve H.Q + 2 Secns 61st Co. RE H.Q. and 1 Co: Pioneers less 50 O.R. allotted to signal Co: for burying cable	

1577 Wt. W10791/1773 500,000 1/15 D. D. & L. A.D.S.S./Forms/C. 2118.

Instructions regarding War Diaries and Intelligence Summaries are contained in F. S. Regs., Part II. and the Staff Manual respectively. Title pages will be prepared in manuscript.

WAR DIARY
or
INTELLIGENCE SUMMARY.
(Erase heading not required.)

Army Form C. 2118.

Place	Date	Hour	Summary of Events and Information	Remarks and references to Appendices
BELLEVUE FARM	22.8.16	11 am	CRE visited 41st and 42nd Infy: brigades 61st 62nd and 89th Cos: RE and Pioneers	
		8 pm	CRE visited CRE 7th Divn	
"	23.8.16	8.15 am	Adjt. visited trenches in DELVILLE wood.	
		3 pm	CRE visited the field Cos: RE to discuss RE operations during the projected attack on the 24th. RE companies + pioneers allotted to Infy: brigades as on 22nd inst:	2nd Lieut N.S. CLOUSTON RE(TC) joined 61st Co.
		6 pm	Operation order No 78. received. The RE and Pioneers to construct strong points at or near S.12.C.5.9, trench junction T.13.C.95.50; junction of ALE ALLEY and BEER TRENCH; Salient of DELVILLE Wood S.12.d.6.3., Trench junction COCOA LANE and BEER TRENCH. (see map 14th Divn of 23.8.16	2nd Lieut. A PRAIN RE joined 62nd Co.
"	24.8.16	10 am	CRE visited the field Co. RE	
		11 am	Orders received that the attack on trench junction T13.C 95.50 will not take place. Consequently no strong point to be made there.	
		9.20 pm	O.C. 62nd Co. RE reported ~~Infy~~ RE + Pioneers were ordered forward ~~from~~ to S.12C central to make a strong point at or near it at 8.50 pm. One platoon of Pioneers ordered forward to consolidate inner trench at 9.15 pm	
"	25.8.16	1.15 am	2Lt MOWBRAY with one sect. 89th Co. RE and 1 platoon pioneers moved up to make strong point at S.12C5.9.	
		9 am.	Report ~~is~~ received that the 14th Divn now hold all DELVILLE WOOD and join with right of 33rd Divn at junction of TEA trench and FLERS road.	
			Parties of 62nd Co: RE and Pioneers detailed to make strong points for the 41st Brigade were employed as guides for reinforcements and for carrying up Stokes mortar ammunition as the work for which they were detailed could not be carried out.	

Army Form C. 2118.

WAR DIARY
or
INTELLIGENCE SUMMARY.
(*Erase heading not required.*)

Instructions regarding War Diaries and Intelligence Summaries are contained in F. S. Regs., Part II. and the Staff Manual respectively. Title pages will be prepared in manuscript.

Place	Date	Hour	Summary of Events and Information	Remarks and references to Appendices
BELLEVUE FARM	25 8/16	4am	2nd Lieut BOYD CARPENTER, 89th Co RE successfully completed the construction of a strong point in INNER TRENCH. DELVILLE WOOD S12C central. No RE casualties on night 24/25	
"	26 8/16	8.30am	CRE went with OC 61st Co RE to visit trenches in DELVILLE wood. Were held up by artillery fire in ANGLE trench. Enemy were firing on ANGLE trench and the trench west of and parallel to it. Also on SOUTH street. This fire has been practically continuous for 10 hours, and has rendered communication with DELVILLE wood uncertain. Orders received that 22nd Infy Brigade 7th Div will relieve 41st Infy Brigade 14th Div in HOP ALLEY, BEER trench etc. 41st Infy Brigade move to DERNANCOURT night 26/27. Distribution of RE and pioneers will be 89th Co RE with Lein Pioneers with 43rd Infy Brigade holding DELVILLE wood. 61st Co RE to assist 89th Co RE if required. 62nd Co RE and HQ + 2 Cos Pioneers in reserve.	
"	27 8/16	3pm	CRE visited 61st 62nd 89th Co RE and 11th King Liverpool Regt Pioneers to arrange for future work.	
		5pm	43rd Infy Brigade captured a small length of trench in DELVILLE WOOD (the last portion held by the enemy) also a portion of ALE ALLEY adjoining about 50 prisoners taken.	
"	28 8/16	10am	CRE visited the three field companies and Pioneers.	
		1pm	CE XV Corps visited CRE and arranged for employment of 400 New Zealand Pioneers on construction of a communication trench from CRUCIFIX ALLEY to ANGLE TRENCH. Work to be laid out and supervised by OC 61st Co RE. Line of trench approx S18C.6.6. to S18C.8.8. Work to be finished by 29th inst	
		3pm	CRE 24th Div came to consult about taking over on relief of 14th Div by 24th Div	
		5pm	Operation order 40 received. 14th Div to complete the capture of BEER TRENCH on the 30th inst. if this has not been done before. 43rd Infy Brigade to be employed with 2 Cos. Pioneers for consolidation work.	

Instructions regarding War Diaries and Intelligence Summaries are contained in F. S. Regs., Part II. and the Staff Manual respectively. Title pages will be prepared in manuscript.

WAR DIARY
or
INTELLIGENCE SUMMARY.
(Erase heading not required.)

Army Form C. 2118.

Place	Date	Hour	Summary of Events and Information	Remarks and references to Appendices
BELLEVUE FARM	29.8.16	8 a.m.	Report received from 61st Co. R.E. that only 150 yds of Communication trench was dug between CRUCIFIX ALLEY and ANGLE TRENCH on night 28/29. 89th Co. R.E. report no wiring possible in front of INNER TRENCH. The party employed on it lost 2 officers and 10 O.R.	Lieut BOYD CARPENTER killed Lieut MOWBRAY wounded
"	30.8.16	11 a.m.	C.R.E. handed over work to C.R.E. 24th Div. Field Cos: and Pioneers relieved by corresponding units. Field Cos: moved to billets in DERNANCOURT.	
"	31.8.16	11 a.m.	Division moved back to rest by train from EDGEHILL to AIRAINES arrived 4 p.m. C.R.E. to Divl. H.Q. at BELLOY St LAURENT 61st Co. R.E. to BOIRAULT 62nd Co. to AVESLEGES 89th Co. to FRETTECUISE	

O/C

SECRET.

O.C.61st Fd Co.R.E.,
" 62nd "
" 11th Kings Liverpool Regt (Pioneers).

Reference para 6 C.R.E's Operation Order No.5.

Consolidating parties of R.E. and Pioneers will return to their billets on completion of work.

Para 11 of CRE's Operation Order No 5 is cancelled.

J E Carter

Lieut Colonel R.E.,

17/8/16. C.R.E.14th Division.

SECRET. Copy No. 9

14th Division R.E.Operation Order No.5.

Reference 1/10,000 Trench Maps
12 a and b and 13.

17 August
1916.

1. On the 18th August the XIII, XV and III Corps are making a simultaneous attack on the enemy lines.

2.(a)On our right the left flank of the 24th Division has for its objective the trench S 18 d 6.4 to trench junction S 24 b 9.8.

(b)On our left the 33rd Division has for its objective WOOD LANE from our left and HIGH WOOD from S 4 d 2.6 to S 3 b 8.1.

3. The objectives allotted to the 14th Division are:-

(i)S 18 d 6.4 - the angle formed by the German trench at S 18 d 6.5 - T 13 c 4.9 - BEER TRENCH to junction with ALE ALLEY - ALE ALLEY to T 13 a 0.7 - S 18 b 7.9 and thence back to our front line about S 18 b 0.8.

(ii)S 11 d 8.6 - ORCHARD TRENCH - WOOD LANE to S 11 a 3.2

Objective (i) is allotted to the 43rd Inf.Bde. and objective (ii) to the 41st Inf.Bde.

4. The attack will be preceded by a bombardment by the Heavy Artillery as detailed in attached table "A" (to be issued later) and by the Field Artillery as detailed in 5th Div. Operation Order No.35 and 17th Div. Operation Order No.45.

5. Objectives when gained will at once be consolidated. The 41st Inf. Bde. will take steps to join up right of their objective to our present front line.
Strong points will be established in the vicinity of the following points:-

43rd Inf. Bde. (i). enemy salient at S 18 d 6.5. This point must be captured at all costs as it is most important for the success of the left of the 24th Division attack that this point is gained and held by us.

(ii). point where ALE ALLEY enters DELVILLE WOOD.

(iii). junction of German trenches at S 18 b 7.9.

41st Inf. Bde. (i). junction of German trenches about S 11 d 8.6.

(ii). S 11 d 0.8.

(iii). junction of ORCHARD TRENCH and WOOD LANE.

6. For the purpose of assisting in the consolidation of the strong points after they have been occupied and a firm hold obtained by the Infantry, one Field Coy R.E., and one company Pioneers are allotted to each attacking Infantry Brigade. Infantry Brigades to arrange details direct with C.R.E. and O.C.Pioneers.

7. All watches must be very carefully synchronized. The 14th Divisional Signal Coy. will arrange to send out the time at 9 p.m. 17th August and 10 a.m. 18th August.

8.

8. (a). During the night 18/19th August the S.O.S. signal will be one "golden rain" rocket.

(b). For the purposes of identification 43rd Inf. Bde. will fire one "golden rain" rocket from POMMIERS REDOUBT at 9 p.m. on 17th August.

(c). Except on the night 18/19th August the S.O.S. signal will remain the same as that now in force, viz:-
5 red rockets in quick succession.

9. The 41st and 43rd Inf. Bdes. will each be issued with 10 Artillery boards 4 ft by 3 ft and coloured as under.

~~Yellow~~ White / Red

These boards are not to be taken forward by the first attacking troops but are to be sent up after positions have been definitely won and consolidated. These boards are to be erected behind the parados of trenches with the coloured side towards our Artillery.

10. No orders or sketches likely to be of use to the enemy are to be taken into action.

11. ~~Advanced Divisional H.Q. moves to FRICOURT F 3 d 5.2 at 3 p.m. on 18th August.~~ Cancelled.

12. With reference to para 6. the Field Companies R.E., will be allotted as follows:-
61st Co.R.E. to work in 43rd Inf. Bde.Area.
62nd Co.R.E. to work in 41st Inf. Bde.Area.
The O.C.Pioneers will detail one Company for work in the 41st Inf Bde Area. and one company for work in the 43rd Inf. Bde. Area. The Commanders of these Companies should report to O.C.61st Co.R.E. and O.C.62nd Co.R.E. respectively on receipt of this order.

13. The 89th Field Co.R.E., and the Pioneer Battalion, less 2 Cos, will remain in Divisional Reserve ready to move at half hours notice from zero on 18th August.

14. The strong points referred to in para 5 will be large enough to hold a garrison of 1 platoon and provided with emplacements for at least 2 machine guns. They will be constructed for all round defence and will be wired all round.

15. The working parties for each strong point will be one Section R.E. and one platoon Pioneers. From these carrying parties will be detailed to carry stores from the forward dumps to the site of the work.

16. The O.C's 61st and 62nd Cos R.E., will remain at the 43rd and 41st Infantry Brigade Headquarters respectively. They will each retain one Section R.E. and one Platoon Pioneers as a local reserve.

17. The place and time of rendezvous for the Sections R.E. and platoons of Pioneers detailed for consolidation work will be fixed by the O.C's 61st and 62nd Cos R.E. in consultation with the B.G.C.43rd and 41st Infantry Brigades respectively.

18. O.C's 61st and 62nd Cos R.E. will arrange to have all stores required for the consolidation of the strong points dumped before hand near the work.

A supply

A supply of water in petrol tins should be included.

19. On completion of work the R.E. and such of the Pioneers as are not required to garrison the work will return to their rendezvous.

20. When a strong point is completed a report will be sent to the Infantry Brigade concerned and to the C.R.E. and the Infantry in the vicinity should be informed.

Issued at 1.15 a.m.

Lieut Colonel R.E.,

C.R.E.14th Division.

Copy No.
1. 61st Co.R.E.
2. 62nd Co.R.E.
3. 89th Co.R.E.
4. 11th Kings Liverpool Regt (Pioneers.)
5. 41st Inf. Bde.
6. 43rd Inf. Bde.
7. G.S.14th Divn.
8. War Diary.
9. File.

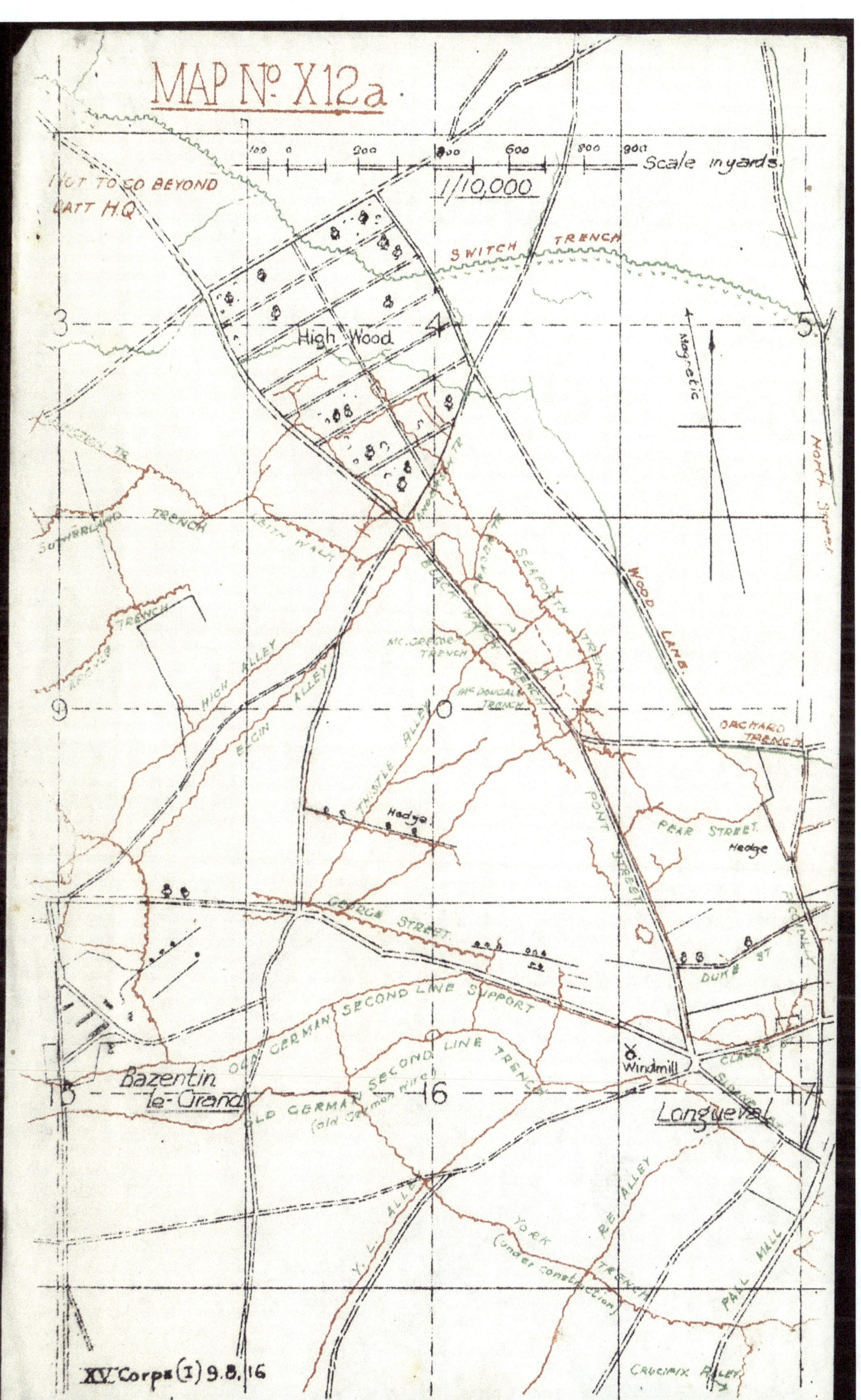
MAP No X12a
Scale in yards.
1/10,000
NOT TO GO BEYOND
BATT H.Q
SWITCH TRENCH
High Wood
Magnetic
SUTHERLAND TRENCH
LEITH WALK
BLACK WATCH TRENCH
SEAFORTH TRENCH
WOOD LANE
ARGYLE TRENCH
HIGH ALLEY
ELGIN ALLEY
THISTLE ALLEY
Mc GREGOR TRENCH
Mc DOUGALL TRENCH
ORCHARD TRENCH
North Street
POINT STREET
PEAR STREET
Hedge
GEORGE STREET
DUKE ST
OLD GERMAN SECOND LINE SUPPORT
OLD GERMAN SECOND LINE TRENCH
(old German wire)
Windmill
Bazentin le-Grand
Longueval
Y. L. ALLEY
YORK TRENCH
(under construction)
RE ALLEY
PALL MALL
CRUCIFIX ALLEY
XV Corps (I) 9.8.16

MAP No. X12.G.
Note. NOT TO GO BEYOND BATT. H.Q.
Scale in yards
Trenches correct to 8.8.16.
Flers.
German Third Line
SWITCH TRENCH
COFFEE LANE
TEA SUPPORT
TEA LANE
TEA TR
NORTH STREET.
COCOA LANE
FLERS ROAD
ORCHARD TRENCH
Delville Wood
PRINCESS STREET
REGENT ST
BOND ST
STRAND
KING ST
ROTTEN ROW
BUCHANAN ST
CAMPBELL ST
Longueval
CLARGES ST
PICCADILLY
HAYMARKET
SOUTH STREET.
(old German line)
DOVER ST
DOWN ST
ANGLE TR
HIGH
PALL MALL
CHEAPSIDE
LONGUEVAL ALLEY
Waterlot Farm
Guinchy
YORK TRENCH
(under construction)
Chy
HOLBORN
Trones Wood.
XV Corps (I) 9.8.16.

MAP No X19

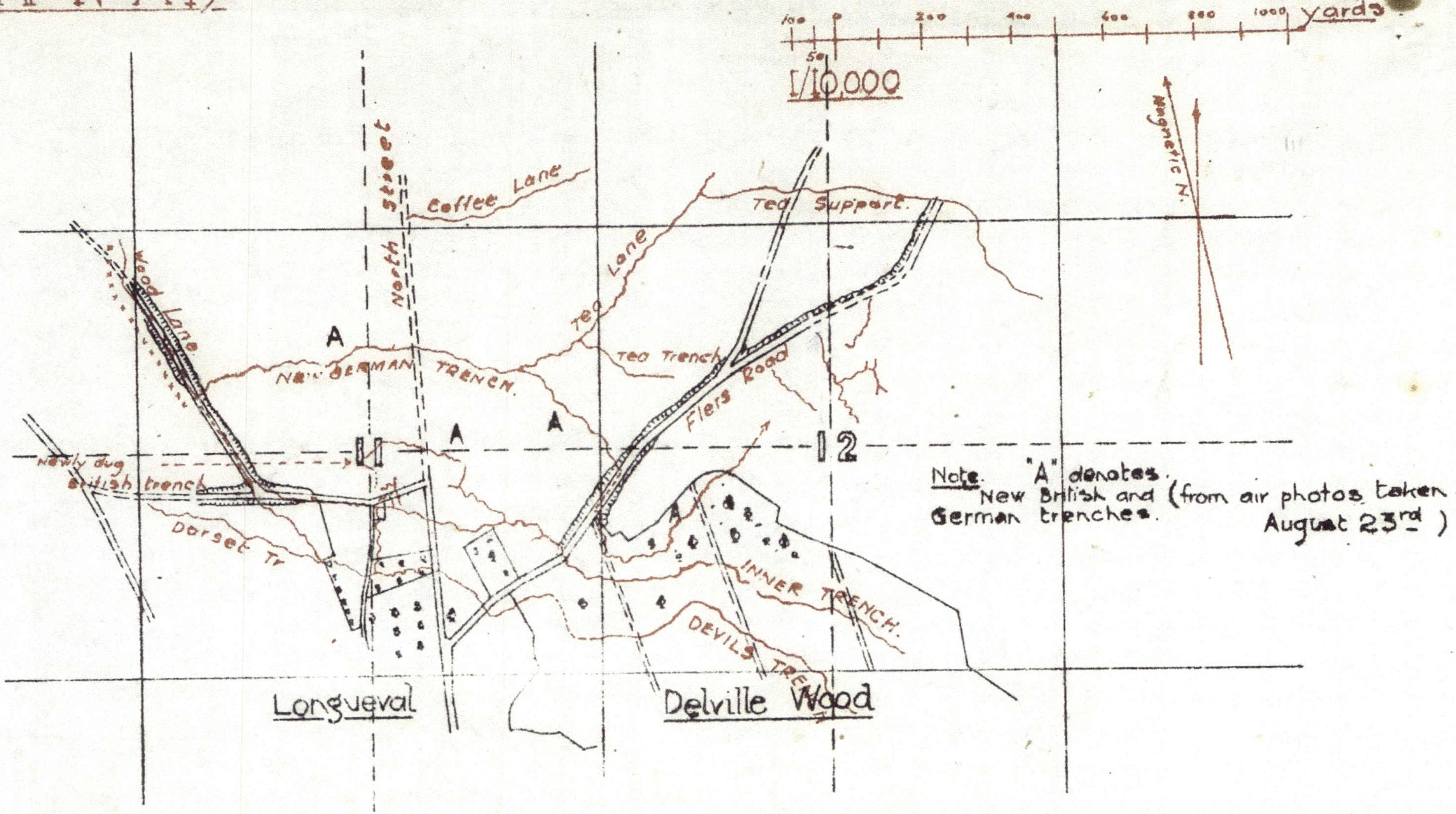

100 50 0 200 400 600 800 1000 Yards

1/10,000

Magnetic N.

Coffee Lane

North Street

Tea Support

Tea Lane

Tea Trench

Flers Road

Wood Lane

New German Trench

A

A

A

11

12

Newly dug British trench

Dorset Tr

Inner Trench

Devils Trench

Longueval

Delville Wood

Note. "A" denotes New British and German trenches. (from air photos taken August 23rd)

XV Corps. (I) 23.8.16

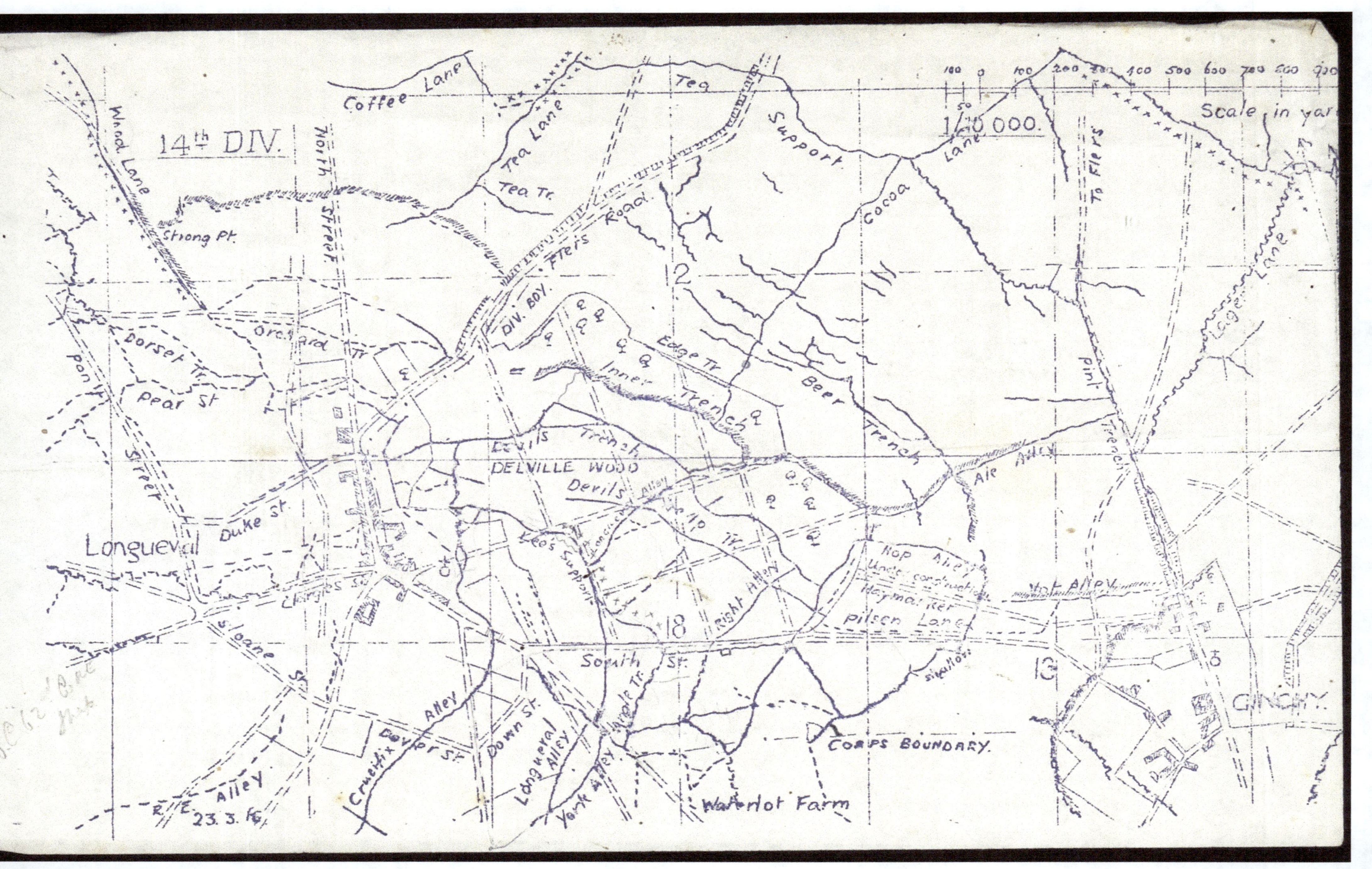
14th DIV.
Scale in yards
1/10 000.
Coffee Lane
Tea Lane
Tea Tr.
Tea
Support
Cocoa
Lager Lane
To Flers
Wood Lane
Strong Pt.
North Street
Flers Road
Div. Bdy.
Orchard Tr.
Dorset Tr.
Pear St
Pont Street
Edge Tr.
Inner Trench
Beer Trench
Pint Trench
Ale Alley
Devils Trench
DELVILLE WOOD
Devils Alley
Hop Alley
Under construction
Haymarket
Pilsen Lane
Stout Alley
Longueval
Duke St.
Clarges St.
Sloane St.
Lees Support
Right Alley
South St.
Swallows
Corps Boundary
Waterlot Farm
Crucifix Alley
Dover St.
Down St.
Longueval Alley
York Alley
Jungle Tr.
R.E. Alley
23.3.16.
Ginchy.
2
7
12
18
13

"A" Form.

Army Form C. 2121.

MESSAGES AND SIGNALS.

No. of Message

Code ..... m.	Words	Charge	This message is on a/c of:	Recd. at ..... m.
Origin and Service Instructions.	Sent		..... Service.	Date
	At ..... m.		O/C	From
	To			
	By		(Signature of "Franking Officer.")	By

	STP SOA SUP	STEP	

Sender's Number.	Day of Month	In reply to Number	AAA
RE127	16		

Ref RE 003 – the stores points will be named as under commencing from South working north west –

S 18 d 6 5		MARS
S 18 b 95 75	(junction ALE ALLEY & Delville Wood)	VENUS
S 18 b 7 9		SATURN
S 11 d 8 5	(junction ORCHARD TRENCH & FLERS RD)	CUPID
S 11 c 10 7		DIANA
S 11 c 5 8	(junction ORCHARD TRENCH & Wood Lane	JUNO

C 89th Cy is painting 8 notice boards for each – 2 plain & 6 with arrows

The stores dumps for these points should be marked with red notice boards painted in white "Reserve for stores points" & all ranks are being warned that these stores should not be touched

The above may be forwarded as now corrected. (Z)

Adjt Div Engr [illegible]

Censor. Signature of Addressor or person authorised to telegraph in his name.

* This line should be erased if not required.

Wt. W14042—M :4. 300000 Pads. 12/15 Sir J. C. & S

"A" Form.

Army Form C. 2121.

MESSAGES AND SIGNALS.

No. of Message ____________

Prefix .... Code .... m.	Words	Charge	This message is on a/c of:	Recd. at .... m.
Office of Origin and Service Instructions.	Sent		.... Service.	Date ....
	At .... m.			From ....
	To			
	By		(Signature of "Franking Officer.")	By ....

TO

Sender's Number.	Day of Month	In reply to Number	AAA

Water supply [illegible]

points will be required [illegible] for a [illegible] station

about 20 [illegible]

[illegible] there are [illegible]

from [illegible] after [illegible] 17th [illegible]

A reserve of stores should be [illegible]

(to which the reserve can be sent in case of

emergency) [illegible]

[illegible]

to supply any [illegible] required.

C.R.E. OFFICE, 14th DIVISION

17 AUG. 1916

[illegible]

From

Place

Time

The above may be forwarded as now corrected. (Z)

Censor. Signature of Addressor or person authorised to telegraph in his name.

* This line should be erased if not required.

(4198) Wt. W14042—M (4. 300000 Pads. 12/15 Sir J. C. & S

O.C.
89th Field Co. R.E.

The following is a report of the work done by No 3 Section, 89th Field Company and No 7 Platoon "B" Coy 11th Kings Liverpools on the night Aug 24th / 25th.

<u>Location of work.</u> Strong Point "A" S 12 c. central.
<u>Hours of work</u> 1.30 am – 4.45 am.
<u>Work done.</u> 5 firebays completed.
2 Machine Gun Emplacements.
point wired all round. Type of wire as per sketch.

No. of men. 5 N.COs 25 Sappers and 35 Kings L'pool Pioneers

A rough sketch of point is attached. There is no scale. The ground slopes down from South to North.

Type of wire used
barbed wire
coil French wire
barbed wire

D Boyd Carpenter
Lt RE

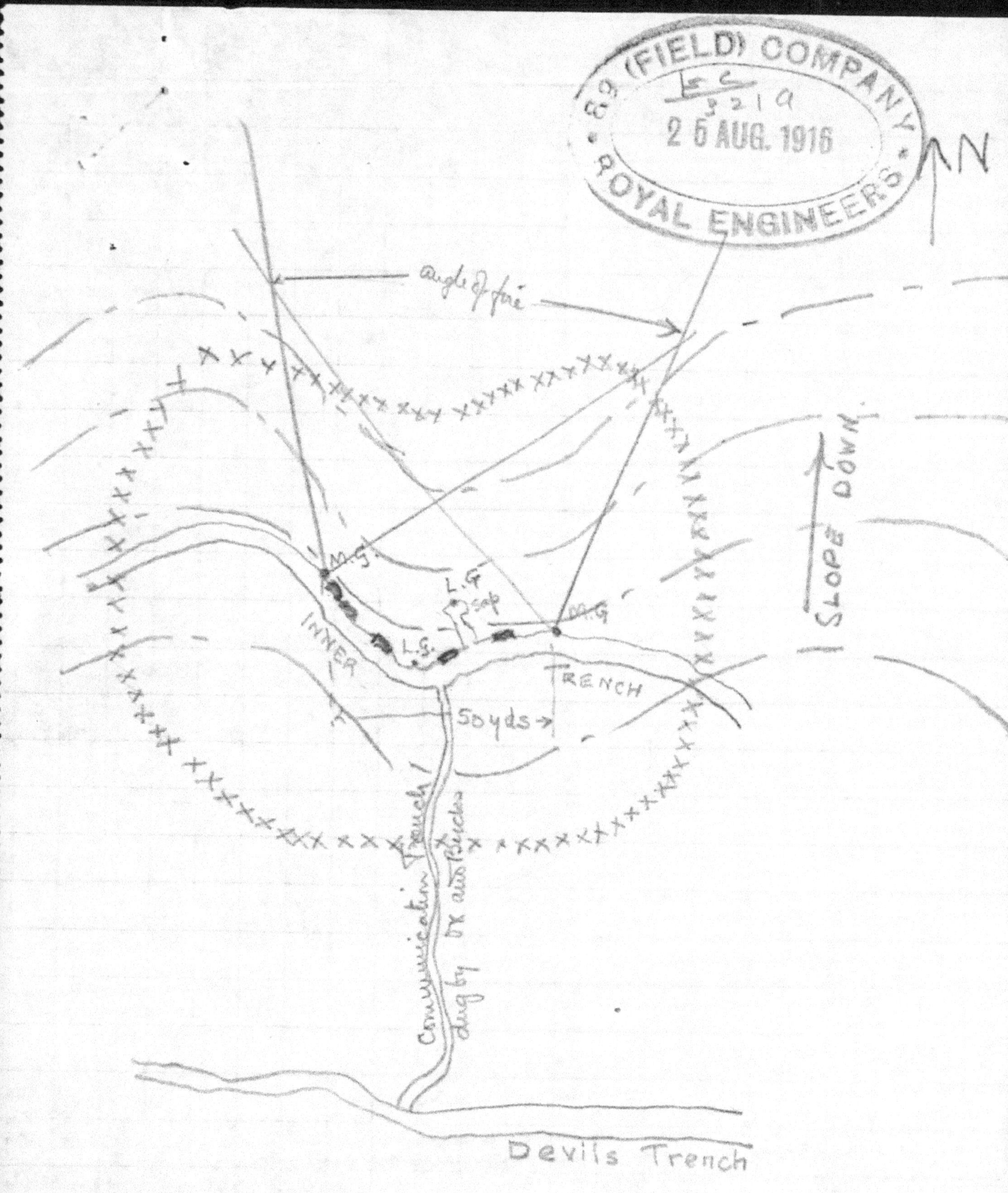

ROUGH SKETCH
SHOWING STRONG POINT "A"
AT S 12 C 5. 5.
NO SCALE.
Aug 25. 1916.

L.G = Lewis Gun
M.G. = Machine Gun
F.B. = Fire BAYS.

barricade made by Infy.

area cleared by Capt Maxwell

WOOD LANE

ORCHARD TRENCH

JUNO

DIANA

20x out from ORCHARD TRENCH

CUPID

FLERS ROAD

area cleared of enemy by infy. line or by outposts shaded blue.

C

A

E

D

15x

30x

FLERS ROAD

Situation at 2a.m. Lewis gun

CUPID.

S.11.d.8.5

B

C.A.R. Chesney Capt. OC 6thy.

19/8/16

bombing post established by attacking Infy. 4 men in.

trench cut by infy.

C.R.E. XIV. Divn.

I have the following points to report with reference to the recent operations. I am reporting from a R.E. point of view entirely.

The whole question of success in the construction of these strong points hangs on the simple fact whether the infantry has got a protecting screen out or not.

In the centre Diana point was constructed exactly as intended. The trench was good & the wire was good. Casualties were slight & due more to misfortune than any deliberate intention on the enemy's part.

In this case the screen consisted of the new line being dug in front of the ORCHARD TRENCH.

On the left Juno, Capt (or Major) MAXWELL had the situation so well in hand that although the strong point was constructed on the extreme left flank

of our front line yet we could work without interruption. Result no ~~[illegible]~~ casualties & the work was got through with despatch.
But this was due entirely to ~~Capt.~~ Major Maxwell's enterprise & care. Some Germans crept up during the night in shell holes etc., & tried to snipe or hunt our men wiring. ~~Capt.~~ Major Maxwell's men immediately set about them & we had no more trouble getting the job through without difficulty.

Lt. Kibby was responsible for carrying ~~the work~~ very well.

On the right however the situation was entirely different. See sketch plan

The Liverpools were struggling to connect up the trench from A to B, being sniped at from ~~[illegible]~~ the immediate right front in DELVILLE WOOD.
Bombs were also being thrown at them. They had lost a large number of their men.
On the arrival of the R.E. officers & wiring parties it was found impossible to shew a hand along the parapet from R to A & D. Any sign of movement would bring 6 to 8 bullets at the

person moving.

My officer cleared up the situation a little & laid out a trench to be dug from C to D.
But before he could see the work completed he was hit.

The R.E. party was at a loss to know what to do – there was not room for them to work from C to D besides the Liverpools digging party. They set about finding ammunition, grenades, & a lost Lewis Gun. A Lewis gun (Liver-pools) was installed at E & the lost one with ammunition was returned to the Infy.

It is to be realised that the sappers got out to wire at C but were bombed. They were then ordered to get into the trench & stand to by the Infy. officers as a bombing attack was feared.

This is a clear example I think of the impossibility of getting a party of 75 as our party was on to constructing a strong point unless there is a screen ~~of~~ covering them.

Either there must be a screen or else the Infy. outposts must have succeeded in driving the enemy's snipers + bombers to arm's length to give room for work.

In this case we were actually trying to construct a strong point in amongst the line of outposts.

Therefore I think the lesson for R.E. is that if the garrison cannot ~~ensure~~ guarantee that the enemy are kept out of bombing distance then the strong point must be constructed behind the line taken up.
For this reason the orders given us as regards the siting of strong points should be elastic + should read "in the neighborhood of ...... behind the furthest line taken up by the infantry after the assault"

A point infantry officers do not realise is that the wire around a point constructed to hold a garrison of 15 men only would generally measure some 120 yards wide by 80 yards deep.

That means one must have clear room for 200 yards by 160 yards, taking 40 yards as bombing distance.

All the difficulties + arguments arising between R.E. + infantry on the matter of the construction of these strong points arises from the lack of recognition of this point. i.e. of dimensions.

I think it is a matter that should be circularised to all so that a right conception of the whole matter may be the foundation of future efforts.

C.W.L. Chesney
Capt. Al.
O.C. 62 Coy. R.E.

19/8/16.

JUNO
Work.
S.11.C.5.8.

German barricade somewhere up. here
shell hole dugout for M.G. Emplt.
WOOD LANE
barricade with L.G.
cover slit
35°
block
gap
gap
ORCHARD TRENCH

Lesson. No digging done by daylight.

Lewis for digging sent up at 3.30 p.m. was ordered by Capt. Prior to stand to as reserve in DORSET TRENCH.

At 12.30 A.M. Capt. Binghamt (Mr Kipp) myself ordered Lt. Hallam to get 20 men out to dig at once.

Meanwhile the reserve platoon 15 men who went up with Lt. Snell Rk. had been digging

Cosy

lewis gun position.

35+

+9

gap

gap

TRENCH.

ORCHARD

proposed communication

DIANA WORK S. 11.d.0.9

No digging was accomplished during daylight by Liverpools sent up at 3.30 p.m.
All digging & wiring was done from dusk onwards.
Directly Liverpools started digging by daylight - a M.G. was turned on to them.

Sketch of SP. MARS

Bombing Post made by S.L.I.

A

gap

40x approx

MG empt

dug out

M.G. empt

B

New trench dug

dugout

dugout

Old German trenches firing outwards.

gap

dugout

C.R.E.

Herewith report on yesterday's operations, as affecting this company.

2. The task of the company was to construct and wire 3 strong points, each for a platoon at

(a) Enemy Salient at S.18.d.6.5. (MARS)

(b) Point where ALE ALLEY enters DELVILLE WOOD (VENUS).

(c) Junction of German trenches at S.18.b.7/9 (SATURN).

3. The necessary stores for each strong point were collected in dumps at S.18.c.7.9, S.18.a.5.3, and S.18.a.5.4, on the night of the 16th: the dumps were inspected on the evening of the 17th by an officer, and arrangements made to make up certain deficiencies.

4 The sections paraded at 6.45 a.m on the 18th instant, picked up their respective platoons of pioneers at POMMIER redoubt, and proceeded to their assembly places as follows.

Section	Assembly Trench	Work
No. 4.	ANGLE Trench	MARS.
No. 1	— ditto —	VENUS
No. 2.	C.T. S.18.a.9½.9 to S.18.a. central.	SATURN.
No. 3	Corps Line, right resting on CRUCIFIX ALLEY.	In reserve.

5. The Brigade instructions were as follows:—
"The Section Officers, R.E. will be responsible for keeping themselves informed of what is happening, and seizing the opportunity of advancing and getting to work. They should not move, however, until the consolidation of the line is well begun".
All the Section Officers showed great determination in pushing forward to find out what was going on: it was while doing this that Lieut BUCKLE was wounded.

6. It was never possible at any time to get any work done on VENUS and SATURN: the enemy being in possession of these points throughout the battle, except for a short period after the assault when I believe the site for VENUS was in our hands, but we were bombed out.
Two sections R.E. and two platoons Pioneers did not therefore succeed in their tasks — they were in cramped trenches close behind the front line from 10 a.m on the 18th. to 4 a.m on the 19th, at times under heavy shell fire.

7. MARS was dug (a rough sketch is attached) and surrounded with a row of French Wire, interlaced with barbed wire.
Time, and the fact that they were crowded with men, prevented us straightening the entering trenches at A and B.

The taping out of the new trench was taken in hand at 3.45 p.m., and, except when interrupted by heavy shelling, work continued until 9 p.m. Sappers and pioneers were hopelessly mixed up with the assaulting infantry, and the greatest difficulty was experienced in getting up stores through the barrage behind the captured line. The first carrying party never reached the strong point at all. The second party, formed by putting sappers on the digging in the strong point instead of pioneers, started 13 strong, and arrived 5 strong. It then became necessary to use some sappers for carrying, the progress of the work slowing down considerably. Eventually, however, the work shown on the sketch was completed.

8. The casualties were very slight – only 10% of the R.E. employed: the section officers showed great judgment in moving their men about to avoid heavy shelling.

9. Generally, from the R.E. point of view, it was a thoroughly unsatisfactory day, only one point out of the three being constructed – the enemy being in possession of the other two sites. The following points came prominently to notice

(a) The infantry working parties must be attached for at least a week beforehand, living with the R.E. company; and getting to know them.

(b) R.E. and working parties should ~~be~~ held not be in any position where they can get mixed up with assaulting troops: the CORPS Line would have been far and away the most suitable place in this case.

(c) A strong point should not be in a line of trenches just captured by infantry — if it is absolutely necessary that it should be, then arrangements must be made for the victorious infantry to evacuate the portion of trench to be converted.

(d) Two ~~section~~ runners per section are necessary.

19/8/16

[signature]
Major R.E.
O.C. 61st Fd Coy RE

B. 208

A.A. & Q.M.G. 14th Divn

I forward herewith war diaries for H.Q. Divl R.E., 61st, 62nd and 89th Field Cos: R.E. for month of Sept: 1916

J.C. Craster
Lt Col RE
CRE 14th Divn

2/10/16

C O N F I D E N T I A L.

W A R
D I AR Y,

of

14TH DIVISIONAL ENGINEERS

for

September 1st 1916 to September 30th .

Instructions regarding War Diaries and Intelligence Summaries are contained in F. S. Regs., Part II. and the Staff Manual respectively. Title pages will be prepared in manuscript.

WAR DIARY
or
~~INTELLIGENCE SUMMARY.~~
(Erase heading not required.)

H.Q. 14th Divl. RE

Army Form C. 2118.

Place	Date	Hour	Summary of Events and Information	Remarks and references to Appendices
BELLOY St LAURENT	1/9/16	10 am	CRE visited 62nd Co. RE at AVESLEGES Pioneers at TAILLY 61st Co. RE at BOIRAULT and 89th Co. RE at FRETTECUISE to arrange programme of training	
"	2/9/16	8.15 am	CRE visited 56th Div near St RIQUIER to see demonstration of heavy machine gun "tanks"	
"	3/9/16	9.30 am	CRE visited 62nd and 89th Cos. RE. Adjutant sick	
"	4/9/16		CRE employed in office adjutant sick. 62nd Co. RE moved from AVESLEGES to VILLERS CAMPEART 1 sec 61st Co RE by lorry to AULT for bathing	
"	5/9/16	9.30 am	CRE visited 61st 62nd and 89th Cos. RE. adjutant sick.	
"	6/9/16	8 am	CRE attended XV Corps conference at HEILLY to discuss roads, water supply, traffic etc in case of an advance.	
"	7/9/16	10.45 am	CRE Inspected 89th Co. RE.	
		2 pm	CRE visited 61st and 62nd Co. RE.	
"	8/9/16	9.30 am	CRE inspected 61st and 62nd Co. RE	
"	9/9/16	7 am	Div Operation Order No 83 recd. 89th Co to move with 41st Brigade Group on 10th 62nd Co RE with 42nd Brigade Group on 11th 61st Co RE with 43rd Brigade Group on 12th to XV Corps area around DERNANCOURT. Div H.Q. to move to BUIRE camp on 11th. Transport to move by road starting one day previous to units. Units (dismounted portion) to move by bus or rail.	
"	10/9/16	11 am	HQ transport left by road for BUIRE 89th Co RE by train to DERNANCOURT. Transport of 62nd Co RE by road for DERNANCOURT	

1577 Wt. W10791/1773 500,000 1/15 D. D. & L. A.D.S.S./Forms/C. 2118.

Instructions regarding War Diaries and Intelligence Summaries are contained in F. S. Regs., Part II. and the Staff Manual respectively. Title pages will be prepared in manuscript.

WAR DIARY
or
INTELLIGENCE SUMMARY.
(Erase heading not required.)

Army Form C. 2118.

Place	Date	Hour	Summary of Events and Information	Remarks and references to Appendices
BELLOY St LAURENT	11	7.0a	Div HQ moved to camp W of BUIRE. 89th Co. RE to FRICOURT CAMP 62nd Co. RE to DERNANCOURT	
		5pm	Operation Order no 84 recd. 41st Infy Brigade to relieve right sector of front held by 41st Div on 12.9.16	
BUIRE	12	9.0a	CRE visited HQ 41st Div ref taking over right brigade sector of DELVILLE WOOD. Afterwards visited 89th Co. RE. 62nd Co RE moved to bivouac in FRICOURT Wood. 61st Co RE to DERNANCOURT.	
BUIRE	13	8.0a	CRE joined Div HQ at FRICOURT. 89th Co. RE moved to FRICOURT.	
		11a	CRE and OC 89th Co. RE visited 41st Infy Brigade at MONTAUBAN to arrange work for RE & Pioneers. Pioneers to dig 2 communication trenches in DELVILLE WOOD and a new trench SE from JAMES STREET	
		5pm	Divl Operation Order no 85 received 14th Divn to take all trenches up to and including GUEUDECOURT assisted by 2 male and 2 female tanks.	
FRICOURT	14	8a	Pioneers got the two communication trenches through to depth of 4 ft. Trench from JAMES street dug SE for 290 yards. Batt HQ in GREEN street commenced.	
		2pm	CRE issued Operation order. Pioneers to make good road west of BERNAFAY wood through LONGUEVAL. 89th Co. to make track for artillery round S and E of DELVILLE WOOD	
"	15.	6.20a	Attack commenced. 2nd Lieut MARGARSON 89th Co. RE wounded night 14/15th in GREEN trench	
		8.30a	2 Secs 89th Co. RE moved forward from S.23.a Central to construct track for artillery from S.12.a.6.4. to T.7 central.	

1577 Wt. W10791/1773 500,000 1/15 D. D. & L. A.D.S.S./Forms/C. 2118.

Instructions regarding War Diaries and Intelligence Summaries are contained in F. S. Regs., Part II. and the Staff Manual respectively. Title pages will be prepared in manuscript.

WAR DIARY
or
INTELLIGENCE SUMMARY.
(Erase heading not required.)

Army Form C. 2118.

Place	Date	Hour	Summary of Events and Information	Remarks and references to Appendices
FRICOURT	15/9/16	10.30 am	Pioneers report road through LONGUEVAL now passable for field artillery.	
		11. Noon	61st Co: R.E. moved to join 43rd Infy: Brigade in area N.E. of MONTAUBAN.	
			Division reached the line M 31 b 4.0. to ~~N32c~~. T 3 a 3.9. attack on GIRD TRENCH, GIRD SUPPORT and GUEUDECOURT postponed owing to divisions on right and left not being up.	
		6.0 pm	Operation Order no 86 received. attack to be continued on 16.9.16. 89th Co: R.E. completed track for artillery from S 12 a 6.4 to T.7 central	
"	16/9/16	4 am	Operation Order no 87 received giving details of attack on GIRD TRENCH, GIRD SUPPORT and GUEUDECOURT. attack to start at 9.25 am.	
		9.25 am	attack reached GIRD TRENCH but had to fall back owing to flanks being exposed.	
		6.30 pm	attack on GIRD TRENCH and GIRD SUPPORT repeated. Reached GIRD TRENCH but had to fall back owing to flanks being exposed	
"	17/9/16	9 am	Div HQ moved back to BUIRE camp. 89th Co RE to RIBEMONT 62nd to area 'A' N of DERNANCOURT 61st Co to DERNANCOURT.	
BUIRE	18/9/16	to 21/9/16	Division resting	
"	22/9/16		Div: moved by bus to LUCHEUX area. Div: H.Q. to LE CAUROY	
LE CAUROY	23/9/16	9 am	C.R.E. visited C.R.E. 12th Div at WARLUS to arrange taking over from 12th Div of F.Q.+H sectors.	

1577 Wt. W10791/1773 500,000 1/15 D. D. & L. A.D.S.S./Forms/C. 2118.

Army Form C. 2118.

Instructions regarding War Diaries and Intelligence Summaries are contained in F. S. Regs., Part II. and the Staff Manual respectively. Title pages will be prepared in manuscript.

WAR DIARY
or
INTELLIGENCE SUMMARY.
(Erase heading not required.)

Place	Date	Hour	Summary of Events and Information	Remarks and references to Appendices
LE CAUROY	24 9/16		CRE employed in office	
"	25 9/16	8.30am	CRE went round work in G sector & part of F sector with CRE 12th Div	
"	26 9/16	9am	CRE moved with Divl HQ to GOUY. 62nd Co: took over work in G sector & moved to AGNY 1 Sec to WARLUS	
GOUY	27	9am	CRE visited CRE 12th Div to take over documents.	
"	28	9am	CRE moved with Divl HQ to WARLUS.	
WARLUS	29	9.30am	CRE visited 61st Co. RE. at LE FERMONT afterwards examined PLANK STREET.	
"	30.	9.30am	CRE visited 42nd Infy Brigade 43rd Infy Brigade 89th Co RE and Pioneer workshop at DAINVILLE	

J. C. Coster? Lt Col RE
CRE 14th Div

1577 Wt. W10791/1773 500,000 1/15 D. D. & L. A.D.S.S./Forms/C. 2118.

Vol 13

Confidential

War Diary

of

14th Divisional Engineers

from 1st Oct 16 to 31st Oct 16.

Army Form C. 2118.

Instructions regarding War Diaries and Intelligence Summaries are contained in F. S. Regs., Part II. and the Staff Manual respectively. Title pages will be prepared in manuscript.

WAR DIARY
or
~~INTELLIGENCE SUMMARY.~~
(Erase heading not required.)

H.Q. 14th Divl. RE

Oct 1916

Place	Date	Hour	Summary of Events and Information	Remarks and references to Appendices
WARLUS	1/10/16	9 am	CRE went round support and reserve line in H sector with B.G.C. 43rd Infy. Brigade and O.C. 89th Co. RE. Very few fire bays and mostly in bad repair.	
"	2/10/16	9.30 am	CRE visited 42nd Infy. Brigade and O.C. 62nd Co. RE. AGNY defences and MILL POST.	
"	3/10/16	9.30 am	CRE visited 61st Co. RE at LE FERMONT. S.O. CE VIth Corps visited CRE to discuss policy of Russian saps in F + G sectors	
"	4/10/16	9.30 am	CRE visited BEAUMETZ, LARBRET workshops, and CRE 46th Div: at BAVINCOURT to discuss the supply of water to trenches in F sector from BRETENCOURT CHATEAU. Afterwards visited [illegible] at BARLY	
"	5/10/16	9 am	CRE visited 89th Co. RE and 43rd and 42nd Infy. brigades.	
"	6/10/16	9.30 am	CRE visited 61st Co. RE and 41st Infy. brigade.	
"	7/10/16	9.0 am	CE VIth Corps visited CRE	
"	8/10/16	9 a.m	CRE proceeded on leave. Relieved by O.C. 62 Coy. RE.	
"	9/10/16	9 a.m	work in office	
"	10/10/16	9 a.m	a/CRE visited 89 Coy + 43rd Bde to see about recesses + arrangements for installation of bombs + smoke candles.	
"	11/10/16	9 am	" visited 62 Coy + inspected Russian saps.	
"	12/10/16	9 a.m	CE VI Corps visited a/g CRE.	

1577 Wt. W10791/1773 500,000 1/15 D. D. & L. A.D.S.S./Forms/C. 2118.

Army Form C. 2118.

Instructions regarding War Diaries and Intelligence Summaries are contained in F. S. Regs., Part II. and the Staff Manual respectively. Title pages will be prepared in manuscript.

WAR DIARY
or
INTELLIGENCE SUMMARY.
(Erase heading not required.)

Place	Date	Hour	Summary of Events and Information	Remarks and references to Appendices
WARLUS	13/10/16	9 a.m.	O/C CRE inspected tramlines G + F sectors with CE VI Corps.	
"	14/10/16	9 a.m.	O/C CRE visited 61 + 62 Coys with reference to Russian saps.	
"	15/10/16	9 a.m.	O/C CRE visited WANQUETIN, BERNEVILLE.	
"	16/10/16	9 a.m.	O/C CRE visited DAINVILLE, parks.	
"	17/10/16	9 a.m.	O/C CRE office. CRE returned from leave. 8 pm.	
"	18/10/16	9 a.m.	O/C CRE visited BERNEVILLE reference report + estimate for extra accommodation.	
"	19.10.16	9.15 am	CRE visited 69th Co. RE and dugouts in H. sector.	
"	20.10.16	9.15 am	CRE visited 61st Co. RE and tramway and dugouts in F sector	
"	21.10.16	9.30 am	CRE visited 4th Batt. Special Brigade RE to arrange about putting in new pattern [illegible] along the Divl. front.	
"	22.10.16	10 am	CRE visited LARBRET workshops and work at BARLY and WANQUETIN.	
"	23.10.16	9.30 am	CRE visited GOWER St, AGNY, MILL POST and GRANTHAM St.	
"	24.10.16		CRE employed in office	
"	25.10.16		— do — O.C. 4th Bn Special Brigade visited CRE. Relief of 14th Div Infy by 12th Div commenced	
"	26.10.16	9 am	CE VIth Corps visited CRE	
		2 pm	CRE visited BERNEVILLE and examined pumps. Relief of 14th Div Infy by 12th Div completed night of 26/27th.	

1577 Wt. W10791/1773 500,000 1/15 D. D. & L. A.D.S.S./Forms/C. 2118.

Army Form C. 2118.

Instructions regarding War Diaries and Intelligence Summaries are contained in F. S. Regs., Part II. and the Staff Manual respectively. Title pages will be prepared in manuscript.

WAR DIARY
or
INTELLIGENCE SUMMARY.
(Erase heading not required.)

Place	Date	Hour	Summary of Events and Information	Remarks and references to Appendices
WARLUS	27/10/16	10am	G.O.C. 12th Div. took over command of sector. R.E. R.A. and Pioneers of 14th Div. remain in the sector and come under orders of G.O.C. 12th Div.	
"	28.10.16		C.R.E. employed in office	
	29th	2pm	C.R.E. visited 35th and 36th Infy. brigades and 89th Co R.E. at ARRAS. afterwards visited O.C. pioneers at BERNEVILLE. 2 Cos. Infy of 9th Div. allotted for work in each brigade sector, and 2 Cos. for work under O.C. Pioneers on main communication trenches. Also 2 Secns R.E. 9th Div for work in G sector and 2 for work in H sector. Work to commence on 1st Nov.	
	30	9am	C.E. VIth Corps visited C.R.E.	
		12 noon	C.R.E. visited O.C. Pioneers BERNEVILLE to arrange work on main communication trenches.	
		5.30pm	O.C. 63rd Co. R.E. 9th Div reported arrival of his Co. in ARRAS. 12 men allotted to F sector. Sec of Pontoon Park arrived at LARBRET.	
	31st		C.R.E. visited 61st Co. R.E. and O.C. Pioneers also inspected FLANK STREET.	

J.C. Rhodes[?] Lt Col RE
CRE 14th Div

1577 Wt. W10791/1773 500,000 1/15 D. D. & L. A.D.S.S./Forms/C. 2118.

Army Form C. 2118.

Instructions regarding War Diaries and Intelligence Summaries are contained in F. S. Regs., Part II. and the Staff Manual respectively. Title pages will be prepared in manuscript.

WAR DIARY

~~or~~

~~INTELLIGENCE SUMMARY.~~

(Erase heading not required.)

Vol 14

Place	Date	Hour	Summary of Events and Information	Remarks and references to Appendices
			Confidential War Diary of Headquarters, 14th Div! Engineers. from 1st November 1916 to 30th November 1916 Volume I	

1577 Wt. W10791/1773 500,000 1/15 D. D. & L. A.D.S.S./Forms/C. 2118.

Instructions regarding War Diaries and Intelligence Summaries are contained in F. S. Regs., Part II. and the Staff Manual respectively. Title pages will be prepared in manuscript.

Army Form C. 2118.

WAR DIARY
or
~~INTELLIGENCE SUMMARY.~~ HQ 14th Divl. Engineers

(Erase heading not required.)

1

Place	Date	Hour	Summary of Events and Information	Remarks and references to Appendices
WARLUS	1/11/16	9.30am	CRE visited LARBRET WORKSHOPS.	
		3pm	CRE 12th Div visited CRE 14th to arrange taking over.	
	2/11/16	10am	CRE visited FOX sketch with CRE 12th Div afterwards arranged handing over	
	3rd	9am	CRE preparing to hand over to CRE 12th Div	
	4th	2pm	CRE discussed line for new tramway for heavy TMs in G and H sector with CE VIth Corps and CRE 12th Div.	
	5th	1pm	CRE handed over to CRE 12th Div	
		2pm	CRE moved to GOUY. The 3 field Cos: moved to GOUY on night 5/6th on relief by 12th Div	
GOUY	6th	9.30am	CRE visited Divl HQ 14th Div at LE CAUROY afterwards visited Maire of LIGNEREUIL with a view to purchasing timber in BOIS DE FAYE and BOIS DE RIBERMONT. Found all wood already purchased by ADC 6th Corps for firewood	
GOUY	7th	9.30am	CRE rejoined Divl HQ at LE CAUROY 62nd Co: RE moved to HONVAL	
LE CAUROY	8th	9.30am	CRE visited Maire of HOUVIN to try to arrange purchase of timber.	
	9th	10am	CRE visited Inf. School at GRAND RULLECOURT and 61st Co. RE at GOUY	
	10th	10am	CRE visited BARLY wood to look for brushwood afterwards visited 61st Co RE at GOUY	
	11th	9.30am	CRE visited wood near REBREUVIETTE to find brushwood	

1577 Wt. W10791/1773 500,000 1/15 D. D. & L. A.D.S.S./Forms/C. 2118.

Instructions regarding War Diaries and Intelligence Summaries are contained in F. S. Regs., Part II. and the Staff Manual respectively. Title pages will be prepared in manuscript.

WAR DIARY
or
INTELLIGENCE SUMMARY.

(Erase heading not required.)

Army Form C. 2118.

2

Place	Date	Hour	Summary of Events and Information	Remarks and references to Appendices
LE CAUROY	11	5.30pm	CRE attended a lecture given by Lt Col SINGER RE on employment of RE field Cos (at HESDIN)	
	12.	9am	CRE went to FREVENT to arrange for hire of sawmills. Afterwards went to OCCOCHES to see new sawmill	
	13.		CRE employed in office	
	14	10am	CRE inspected fir wood being cut by ASC near LE CAUROY with a view to taking the larger trees	
	x	3pm	Went with owner to wood at LE CAUROY and marked beech trees for cutting	
	15		CRE employed in office	
	16	10am	CRE visited 89th 62nd and 61st Cos RE	
	17	11.30am	~~CRE~~ CE VIth Corps visited CRE 14th Div to discuss question of [illegible]	
		1pm	CRE visited trench wood cutting party in wood near BERBREUVIETTE. Capt CHESNEY left [illegible] special [illegible] Parks.	
	18	10am	CRE visited 62nd Co RE at IVERGNY and [illegible] CRE at GOUY afterwards visited sawmills at FREVENT	
	19			
	20		CRE employed in office.	
	21.			
	22nd		CRE visited 89th + 62nd Cos RE	
	23rd		CRE visited work at LIENCOURT. 61st Co RE moved to ARRAS to work under 35th + 42nd [illegible]	
	24.		CRE employed in office	

1577 Wt. W10791/1773 500,000 1/15 D. D. & L. A.D.S.S./Forms/C. 2118.

Instructions regarding War Diaries and Intelligence Summaries are contained in F. S. Regs., Part II. and the Staff Manual respectively. Title pages will be prepared in manuscript.

Army Form C. 2118.

3

WAR DIARY
or
INTELLIGENCE SUMMARY.
(Erase heading not required.)

Place	Date	Hour	Summary of Events and Information	Remarks and references to Appendices
LE CAUROY	25.		C.R.E. employed in office.	
– ditto –	26th		Handed over to a/CRE (Major Lees): left for 3rd Army HQ. 2.30 p.m.	
– ditto –	27th		C.R.E. to IVERGNY (62nd Coy) GRAND RULLECOURT, and to SOMBRIN with B.G.C. 41st Bde – Baths, Bunking, 41st Bde Field works School, etc.	
– ditto –	28th		CRE in office –	
– ditto –	29th		To ARRAS (61st Coy RE) in morning – to FREVENT in afternoon (Laundry, Saw mill, etc).	
– ditto –	30th		C.R.E. in office – Water Supply reports for each village in area completed and forwarded.	

E.W. Lees
Major RE
a/CRE. 14th Divn
1. 11. 16

1577 Wt. W10791/1773 500,000 1/15 D. D. & L. A.D.S.S./Forms/C. 2118.

Instructions regarding War Diaries and Intelligence Summaries are contained in F. S. Regs., Part II. and the Staff Manual respectively. Title pages will be prepared in manuscript.

WAR DIARY
or
~~INTELLIGENCE SUMMARY.~~
(Erase heading not required.)

Army Form C. 2118.

H.Q. 14th Divl. RE
December 1916
Vol 15

Place	Date	Hour	Summary of Events and Information	Remarks and references to Appendices
	Dec			
LE CAUROY	1st		O/CRE visited BERLENCOURT, DENIER, LIENCOURT.	
"	2nd	3pm	CRE returned from III Army School	
"	3rd		CRE took over from actg. CRE	
"	4th		Major Lees left to take command of Bridging School at AIRE. CRE selected site for typical	
"	5th		German trenches near GRAND RULLECOURT with GSO1. Attack to be practised against them when dug	
"	5th	9.30am	CRE & Adjt visited GRAND RULLECOURT and SOMBRIN.	
"	6th	2pm	CRE visited HOUVIN and 89th Co RE at SERICOURT afterwards visited sawmill at FREVENT	
"	7th	8.30am	CRE visited entrenching party at GRAND RULLECOURT.	
"	"	4pm	CRE visited C.E. VI Corps to discuss bunking & water supply in the back area.	
"	8th		CRE employed in office. 61st Co. moved from ARRAS to LIGNEREUIL	
"	9th	8.30am	CRE visited entrenching party at GRAND RULLECOURT, 61st Co. at LIGNEREUIL, & work at DENIER and BERLANCOURT	
"	10th		CRE visited AA & QMG VI Corps with AA & QMG 14th Div to discuss accommodation in back area	
"	11th	9.30am	CRE visited HQ 12th Div to arrange relief of 12th Div by 14th Div	
"	12		CRE employed in office.	
"	13th	9.30am	CRE visited CRE 12th Div to arrange taking over the line.	

1577 Wt. W10791/1773 500,000 1/15 D. D. & L. A.D.S.S./Forms/C. 2118.

Instructions regarding War Diaries and Intelligence Summaries are contained in F. S. Regs., Part II. and the Staff Manual respectively. Title pages will be prepared in manuscript.

WAR DIARY
or
INTELLIGENCE SUMMARY.
(Erase heading not required.)

Army Form C. 2118.

Place	Date	Hour	Summary of Events and Information	Remarks and references to Appendices
LE CAUROY	14th	11 am	CRE visited FREVENT sawmill and woods at REBREUVIETTE + LE CAUROY with CRE 12th Divn.	
	15th		CRE employed in office	
	16th		— do —	
	17th		— do —	
	18th		— do —	
	19th	8 am	CRE took over from CRE 12th Divn. and moved to WARLUS	
WARLUS		6 pm	CRE visited CE VIth Corps to ask for wood metal + mine sheeting. None available	
WARLUS	20th	9.30 am	CRE visited 89th Co. RE in ARRAS afterwards inspected work in H sector	
		2 pm	CRE visited 203rd Co. RE in ARRAS and 43rd Infy. Brigade.	
"	21st	9 am	CRE visited workshops at DAINVILLE and trench tramway in G. sector with OC 62nd Co. RE afterwards visited 42nd Infy. Brigade	
"	22nd		CRE employed in office	
"	23rd	9 am	CRE visited 61st Co RE at LE FERMONT	
"	24th	11.30 am	CRE held a conference of Field Co. commanders	
"	25th		CRE employed in office	

Army Form C. 2118.

WAR DIARY
or
INTELLIGENCE SUMMARY.
(Erase heading not required.)

Instructions regarding War Diaries and Intelligence Summaries are contained in F. S. Regs., Part II. and the Staff Manual respectively. Title pages will be prepared in manuscript.

Place	Date	Hour	Summary of Events and Information	Remarks and references to Appendices
WARLUS	26	9.30am	CRE visited 89th Co. RE. – ARRAS and 43rd Infy. Brigade	
	27	9.15am	CRE visited 62nd Co. RE. at AGNY	
	28th	9.30am	CRE visited 61st Co. at LE FERMONT and 41st Infy. Brigade	
	29th		CRE employed in office	
	30th	9 am	CRE visited 89th Co. RE. and 43rd Infy. brigade also trench tramway in H Section	
	31st	10 am	CRE visited CE. VIIth Corps. to discuss transfer of 14th Divn to VIIth Corps.	

J.E. Christie[?] Lt Col RE
CRE 14th Divn.

1577 Wt. W10791/1773 500,000 1/15 D. D. & L. A.D.S.S./Forms/C. 2118.

C O N F I D E N T I A L

War Diaries

of

C.R.E.14th Divn., 61st, 62nd & 89th Fd Cos' R.E.,

From 1. 1. 17 to 31. 1. 17.

****

Instructions regarding War Diaries and Intelligence Summaries are contained in F. S. Regs., Part II. and the Staff Manual respectively. Title pages will be prepared in manuscript.

HQ. 14th Divl RE

WAR DIARY
or
~~INTELLIGENCE SUMMARY.~~
(Erase heading not required.)

January 1917

Army Form C. 2118.

Place	Date	Hour	Summary of Events and Information	Remarks and references to Appendices
WARLUS.	1.1.17		CRE employed in office. CE VIth Corps visited CRE	
	2.1.17	9.30am	CRE visited 62nd Co RE. DAINVILLE workshops and 42nd Infy. Brigade.	
	3.1.17	9.30am	CRE visited 61st Co. RE. and 41st Infy. Brigade	
	4.1.17		CRE employed in office	
	5.1.17	10 am	CRE visited 89th Co RE. and 43rd Infy. Brigade	
	6.1.17	3.8pm	In conjunction with 9th Div on the left, party of 150 of D.L.I. raided enemy lines in daylight, accompanied by 2 RE NCO's to blow up heavy minenwerfer. Owing to defective wirecutting & enemy flank bombing attacks these men only reached German 1st line, where they helped to repulse bombing attacks.	
	8th		C.R.E. proceeded on leave. Maj. E G Alabaster Cdg 89th Fd Co took over duties. Division passes into 7th Corps (C.E. Brig. Gen. Tanner RE) at 10 am	
	9th		O/CRE. visits H Sector of Divl Front. Preparations for carrying up large quantities of gas cylinders postponed, but considerable work necessary to render up C.T's passable for parties carrying these heavy objects. Special Coys RE propose to use tramways on part of the front, & therefore assist in clearing falls &c due to recent wet weather.	
			Considerable amount of time ~~wasted~~ lost owing to lack of wooden sheeting for mined dugouts: of which there are 15 in process of construction. Requisitions in ARRAS & salvage of old dugouts provide material pending arrival of more timber from Base.	

1577 Wt. W10791/1773 500,000 1/15 D. D. & L. A.D.S.S./Forms/C. 2118.

Instructions regarding War Diaries and Intelligence Summaries are contained in F. S. Regs., Part II. and the Staff Manual respectively. Title pages will be prepared in manuscript.

WAR DIARY

or

INTELLIGENCE SUMMARY.

(Erase heading not required.)

Army Form C. 2118.

Place	Date	Hour	Summary of Events and Information	Remarks and references to Appendices
	9th contd.		Camouflage Officer from Special Works Park RE, having finished erecting O.P's in left & centre ~~Divisional~~ Brigade sectors, proceeds to right sector to complete work in hand there. Rate of progress, 2 OP's per night, working party 2 sappers & 6 to 8 Inf. The design of OP's is somewhat heavy: ~~they~~ the next ones will be lighter.	
			Work on Heavy trench Mortar tramway held up as regards widening of trench ~~and~~ & revetting owing to lack of working party. Rail-laying continues. Arrangements made to conceal branches leading to gun positions, advantage being taken of the presence of the camouflage Officer in the area. When complete there will be 11 miles of tramway in Divisional Sector. Suggestions have been invited as to a check or signal system for working the line in order to prevent trucks meeting between passing places. No simple & reliable solution apparent. A loading gauge is fixed to which all lines ~~must~~ must be made to conform within a month. This loading gauge permits of stretcher trucks holding 3 men or the HTM gun truck to pass: Construction of a petrol tractor commenced, same being supplied from Base.	

1577 Wt. W10791/1773 500,000 1/15 D. D. & L. A.D.S.S./Forms/C. 2118.

Instructions regarding War Diaries and Intelligence Summaries are contained in F. S. Regs., Part II. and the Staff Manual respectively. Title pages will be prepared in manuscript.

WAR DIARY
or
INTELLIGENCE SUMMARY.
(Erase heading not required.)

Army Form C. 2118.

Place	Date	Hour	Summary of Events and Information	Remarks and references to Appendices
	10th		a/CRE visited right sector. Company of Pioneers detailed for work on roads by order of Corps. Serious shortage of labour prevents work being carried on on any new construction: & lack of revetting materials & ~~long~~ long length of front held prevent adequate repairs to existing trenches. Help of the Special Bde RE invaluable. Adjt visits trench tramway.	
	11th		a/CRE visits centre sector. Adjt visits ARRAS & 5 chamber dugout under construction by the Infantry Brigade Pioneer Coy. This dugout somewhat damp ~~[illegible]~~ but no trouble anticipated as it is solid chalk. Headcover 25 ft minimum. Small jobs in hand considerably hampered by lack of a light box car to fetch small stores required for completion.	
	13		CE 7th Corps visits a/CRE & goes round part of centre & left sectors. Orders received for reconnaissance of 20 Heavy & 50 Medium T.M. emplacements in left sector: & for the ~~construction~~ reconnaissance & construction by Jan 20th of 4 Heavy & 10 Medium emplacements in right sector	
	14	11 am	½ Coy RE & 2 Coys Inf applied for for work in right sector on above emplacements & for similar number ultimately in left sector.	

1577 Wt. W10791/1773 500,000 1/15 D. D. & L. A.D.S.S./Forms/C. 2118.

Instructions regarding War Diaries and Intelligence Summaries are contained in F. S. Regs., Part II. and the Staff Manual respectively. Title pages will be prepared in manuscript.

WAR DIARY
or
INTELLIGENCE SUMMARY.
(Erase heading not required.)

Army Form C. 2118.

Place	Date	Hour	Summary of Events and Information	Remarks and references to Appendices
	14	7pm	Notified that no extra labour available. 1 Section RE ordered to withdraw from each of the other sectors, & a Pioneer Coy from centre sector, in order to do above work. Personnel of T.M. Batteries & certain RE labour withdrawn from other work in F Sector also available. The latter commence work 15th: parties from other sector 16th. Shortage of material for camouflage (wire netting)	
	15th		a/CRE visits right sector to arrange details of T.M. emplts. with O.C. RE Coy ~~billeted~~ there.	
	16		Orders received to ~~dig~~ mark out & scratch pattern trenches for a raid. a/CRE & O.C. Pioneers visit F Sector & BGC 91st Inf Bde. Ground for pattern trenches reconnoitred in afternoon & laid out following day	
	17		Adjt visits F Sector to report on progress of T.M. emplacements. Work well in hand & will be completed by the time given	
		4pm	OC 181st Tunnelling Coy RE visits RE HQ & gives details of dugouts he ~~was~~ has been ordered to build. One Battalion working party required: we applied General Staff for this. No hope of getting it unless supplied by Corps, as already one Coy of Pioneers & the bulk of battalion in Divl reserve are employed extra-divisionally.	
		4.30	CRE 20th Divn & another RE officer arrive with a view to ascertaining infn	

Instructions regarding War Diaries and Intelligence Summaries are contained in F. S. Regs., Part II. and the Staff Manual respectively. Title pages will be prepared in manuscript.

WAR DIARY
or
INTELLIGENCE SUMMARY.
(Erase heading not required.)

Army Form C. 2118.

Place	Date	Hour	Summary of Events and Information	Remarks and references to Appendices
	17 contd		about the trenches. Arranged that an officer shall be attached to 62nd Coy for this purpose, reporting following day. Snow fell	
	18		Car obtained for assistant adjt to proceed to AMIENS, to obtain saws which have been awaiting collection for 3 weeks. Work in the parks seriously hampered owing to lack of these saws. Adjt & o/c [illegible] employed in office.	
			C.R.E. returns from leave. Frost	
	19.		CRE visits HQ C inf Sector & Fd Coy commander reference details of a raid. Practice trenches practically complete. CRE 30th Divn with adjt & representatives of field Coys & visited sites for certain dugouts & emplacements; also arranged billets for his Coys. Hard frost	
	20		CRE employed in office. RE band arrived — WARLUS Hard frost	
	21.		CRE visited 89th Co. RE in ARRAS. & 43rd Brigade Hard frost	
	22	1.30pm	CRE went to VIIth Corps HQ to take over duties of Chief Engineer VIIth Corps in addition to his own. Hard frost	
	23		CRE employed in office Hard frost	
	24			
	25	9.30am	CRE visited 42nd Brigade DAINVILLE and 62nd Co. RE at AGNY Hard frost	

1577 Wt. W10791/1773 500,000 1/15 D. D. & L. A.D.S.S./Forms/C. 2118.

Army Form C. 2118.

WAR DIARY
or
INTELLIGENCE SUMMARY.
(Erase heading not required.)

Instructions regarding War Diaries and Intelligence Summaries are contained in F. S. Regs., Part II. and the Staff Manual respectively. Title pages will be prepared in manuscript.

Place	Date	Hour	Summary of Events and Information	Remarks and references to Appendices
WARLUS	26	10 am	CRE visited 42nd Infy. Brigade and Pioneer workshops at DAINVILLE. Afterwards visited 89th Co. RE in ARRAS. Hard frost	
	27	10 am	CRE attended Divl. conference	
	"	3 pm	CRE went to CE. VIIth Corps office at FOSSEUX. Hard frost	
	28.	9 am	CRE visited 41st Infy. Brigade and 61st Fd. Co. RE. Hard frost	
	29.	9.30 am	CRE & Adjt. reconnoitred a route for a new tramway from ARRAS-DOULLENS road to the Doctor's House with GSO, afterwards visited 43rd Infy. Brigade. Hard frost	
	30	10 am	CRE visited 42nd Infy. Brigade and 89th Co. RE	
		3 pm	CRE went to CE. VIIth Corps office at FOSSEUX. Some snow fell.	
	31st		CRE employed in office. Hard frost	

J E Craster [?] Lt Col RE.
CRE 14th Div.

1577 Wt. W10791/1773 500,000 1/15 D. D. & L. A.D.S.S./Forms/C. 2118.

2

WAR DIARY
or
~~INTELLIGENCE~~ SUMMARY. H.Q. 14th Divl. R.E.

(Erase heading not required.)

Vol 17

Army Form C. 2118.

Instructions regarding War Diaries and Intelligence Summaries are contained in F. S. Regs., Part II. and the Staff Manual respectively. Title pages will be prepared in manuscript.

Place	Date	Hour	Summary of Events and Information	Remarks and references to Appendices
WARLUS	1/2/17	9.30am	CRE visited 89th Co RE New Zealand Tunnelling Co and 181st Tunnelling Co RE in ARRAS. Inspected work on two advanced Brigade H.Q.s and holes in RONVILLE Road.	continuous hard frost.
	2.		CRE handing over F sector to CRE 49th Divn	
	3.		61st Co. RE moved from LE FERMONT to ARRAS. 62nd Co. RE employed on Arty. Positions under Arty.	
	4.		CRE handing over G sector to CRE 30th Divn	
	5.		CRE visited 43rd Infy. Brigade with G.S.O. 1, afterwards inspected CHRISTCHURCH Cave with a view to selecting new Brigade H.Q.	
	6.		CRE employed in office	
	7th	10am	CRE visited 42nd + 43rd Brigades and 61st 89th and Pioneers in ARRAS	
			62nd Co. RE moved to ARRAS.	
	8th		CRE employed in office	
	9th		CRE visited 42nd Brigade Pioneers and 89th Co. RE in ARRAS. Inspected work in trenches round ARRAS	
	10th	10am	CRE attended Divl. Conference.	
	11th		CRE visited infantry parties working on railways for D.L.R. & railway Cos.	
	12th		CRE visited 42nd + 43rd Infy. Brigades 61st 62nd + 89th Cos. RE and 179th Tunnelling Co RE also workshops at DAINVILLE	

1577 Wt. W10791/1773 500,000 1/15 D. D. & L. A.D.S.S./Forms/C. 2118.

Instructions regarding War Diaries and Intelligence Summaries are contained in F. S. Regs., Part II. and the Staff Manual respectively. Title pages will be prepared in manuscript.

WAR DIARY
or
INTELLIGENCE SUMMARY.
(Erase heading not required.)

Army Form C. 2118.

Place	Date	Hour	Summary of Events and Information	Remarks and references to Appendices
WARLUS	12 2/17	2pm	CRE visited Infy. party working on railway at BERNEVILLE	
	13 2/17	9.30am	CRE attended conference at 14th Div H.Q. to arrange work programme. CE & B.G.G.S VII Corps present.	
	14 2/17		CRE employed in office. Slight thaw.	
	15 2/17	11am	CRE attended conference of Brigadiers at D.H.Q.	
	16 2/17	9.30am	CRE visited 42nd & 43rd Infy Brigades 61st & 89th Cos. R.E. and Pioneers. Inspected work being carried out by 89th Co. R.E.	
	17 2/17	2pm	CRE visited working party on new railway near BERNEVILLE	
	18 2/17	11.30am	CRE attended lecture by Col FOULKES R.E. on offensive use of gas	
	19 2/17	9am	CRE visited 42nd & 43rd Infy. Brigades 61st 62nd & 89th Cos R.E. and 11th Kings Liverpool Regt. Afterwards visited circular trench round ARRAS and DAINVILLE workshops	
	20 2/17		CRE employed in office	
	21 2/17	9.30am	CRE visited 42nd and 43rd Infy. Brigades 61st 62nd & 89th Co. R.E. inspected trench mortar emplacements off HAMILTON and HULL streets	
	22 2/17		CRE employed in office	
	23 2/17	11am	CRE visited Trench mortar emplacements and work generally with CE VII Corps and O.C. 89th Co. R.E.	

Army Form C. 2118.

Instructions regarding War Diaries and Intelligence Summaries are contained in F. S. Regs., Part II. and the Staff Manual respectively. Title pages will be prepared in manuscript.

WAR DIARY
or
INTELLIGENCE SUMMARY.
(Erase heading not required.)

Place	Date	Hour	Summary of Events and Information	Remarks and references to Appendices
WARLUS	24 2/17	11am	CRE attended Divl. conference.	
"	25 2/17		CRE employed in office	
"	26 2/17	9.30am	CRE visited 42nd and 43rd Infy brigades 61st 89th Co. RE and Pioneers. afterwards visited DAINVILLE RE park.	
"	27 2/17		CRE employed in office. Lieut LOVELL joined 62nd Co. RE as a reinforcement vice 2nd Lt KING	
"	28 2/17		CRE visited 61st Co. RE and inspected tramway in HALIFAX St. and dressing station in HUNTER St. afterwards visited 42nd + 43rd Brigades and 179th Tunnelling Co. RE.	

[illegible]
Lt Col RE
CRE 14th Div

1577 Wt. W10791/1773 500,000 1/15 D. D. & L. A.D.S.S./Forms/C. 2118.

Vol 18

CONFIDENTIAL.

War Diaries

of

H.Q.14th Divl Engineers, ~~61st, 62nd,~~ & 89 Fd Cos' R.E.,

From/ 1st March.17. To/ 31st March.17.

****

Instructions regarding War Diaries and Intelligence Summaries are contained in F. S. Regs., Part II. and the Staff Manual respectively. Title pages will be prepared in manuscript.

WAR DIARY
or
~~INTELLIGENCE SUMMARY.~~
(Erase heading not required.)

Army Form C. 2118.

H.Q. 14th Divl. Engineers March 1917

Place	Date	Hour	Summary of Events and Information	Remarks and references to Appendices
WARLUS.	1.		CRE employed in office. 5pm visited C.E. VII Corps. at FOSSEUX	
	2.		CRE visited 89th Co. RE & inspected work on signal dugouts, [illegible] and ACHICOURT bridge visited 11th Kings Liverpool 42nd and 43rd Infy. Brigades	
	3.	11 a.m.	CRE attended Divl. conference	
	4.		CRE employed in office	
	5.		CRE visited 43rd Infy. Brigade 179th Tunnelling Co. RE 61st and 62nd Cos RE visited gun positions in stone masons yard. visited 11th Kings Liverpool Regt. saw ACHICOURT BRIDGE	
	6.		CRE visited 42nd & 43rd Infy. Brigades 61st & 62nd Cos. RE & 89th Co. RE	
	7.		CRE visited 42nd & 43rd Infy. Brigades 61st and 89th Cos RE	
	8.		CRE employed in office	
	9.		CRE visited 42nd & 43rd Infy. Brigades 61st & 89th Cos. RE & 11th Kings Liverpool (Pioneers). Selected sites of new communication trenches to the exits of Christchurch Cave.	
	10		CRE attended Divl. Conference	
	11.		CRE employed in office	
	12.		CRE visited 42nd & 43rd Brigades 179th Tunnelling Co 89th Co and 11th Kings	
	13.		CRE employed in office	

1577 Wt. W10791/1773 500,000 1/15 D. D. & L. A.D.S.S./Forms/C. 2118.

Instructions regarding War Diaries and Intelligence Summaries are contained in F. S. Regs., Part II. and the Staff Manual respectively. Title pages will be prepared in manuscript.

WAR DIARY
or
INTELLIGENCE SUMMARY.
(Erase heading not required.)

Army Form C. 2118.

1917

Place	Date	Hour	Summary of Events and Information	Remarks and references to Appendices
BARLUS	14/3/17	9.30 am	CRE visited 42nd & 43rd Infy. Brigades 89th Co. RE and 11th Kings Liverpool Regt afterwards visited RE workshops at DAINVILLE	
	15/3/17	9.30 am	CRE visited 42nd & 43rd Infy. Brigades 179th Tunnelling Co. RE 89th & 61st Co. RE and 11th Kings Liverpool Regt.	
	16/3/17	10.15 am	CRE walked over line of proposed tramway W. of CITADELLE ARRAS with CE VIIth Corps and CRE 56th Div. afterwards inspected trenches near RONVILLE water towers with CE VIIth Corps. 56th Div took over work in H1 sector.	
	17/3/17	10 am	CRE attended Divl. Conference.	
		2 pm	CRE saw OC 3rd Field Squadron with refs to cavalry tracks in H sector	
	18/3/17	10 am	Information received that right Div. of VIIth Corps had occupied German front line trenches. RE Cos. and 2 Cos. of 11th Kings Liverpool Regt Pioneers ordered to concentrate at their billets and prepare for road work.	
		2 pm	43rd Infy. Brigade reported to have sent over 2 companies into German trenches. 179th Tunnelling Co. RE ordered to break out from GODLEYS AVENUE. Pioneers to send 1 Officer and 25 OR to dig trench from the exit of GODLEYS AVENUE to German front line.	
	19/3/17		Div. now occupying German trenches opposite H sector. Germans in TILLOY, the HARP	

1577 Wt. W10791/1773 500,000 1/15 D. D. & L. A.D.S.S./Forms/C. 2118.

Instructions regarding War Diaries and Intelligence Summaries are contained in F. S. Regs., Part II. and the Staff Manual respectively. Title pages will be prepared in manuscript.

WAR DIARY
or
INTELLIGENCE SUMMARY.
(Erase heading not required.)

Army Form C. 2118.

Place	Date	Hour	Summary of Events and Information	Remarks and references to Appendices
WARLUS			and NEUVILLE VITASSE. RE + Pioneers employed on making good roads to the front.	
	20.3/17	9.30am	CRE visited 42nd + 43rd Infy Brigades 61st 62nd + 89th Co. RE 179th Tunnelling Co RE and 11th Kings Liverpool Regt visited new light railway west of ARRAS citadel with CE VII Corps.	
	21 3/17		CRE employed in office Lieut LOVELL 62nd Co RE wounded	
	22 3/17	9.30am	CRE visited 42nd + 43rd Infy Brigades 61st 62nd + 89th Co RE and 11th Kings Liverpool Regt afterwards visited BEAURAINS. Lieut: LOVELL died of wounds.	
	23 3/17		CRE employed in office	
	24 3/17		CRE visited 42nd + 43rd Infy Brigades 61st 62nd + 89th Co RE and 11th Kings Liverpool Regt.	
	25 3/17		CRE employed in office 41st Infy Brigade relieved 42nd + 43rd in the line. Lieut PRESCOTT 89th Co RE wounded	
	26 3/17		CRE visited 41st Infy Brigade 61st 62nd + 89th Co. RE and 11th Kings Liverpool Regt. Afterwards visited RE workshops DAINVILLE	
	27 3/17		CRE employed in office	
	28 3/17		CRE visited 41st Infy Brigade 61st 62nd and 89th Co RE 179th Tunnelling Co RE and 11th Kings Liverpool Regt afterwards visited BEAURAINS Lieut: HALLEY 62nd Co. RE wounded.	
	29 3/17		CRE attended Divl conference 89th Co RE moved to DAINVILLE for training.	

1577 Wt. W10791/1773 500,000 1/15 D. D. & L. A.D.S.S./Forms/C. 2118.

Army Form C. 2118.

Instructions regarding War Diaries and Intelligence Summaries are contained in F. S. Regs., Part II. and the Staff Manual respectively. Title pages will be prepared in manuscript.

WAR DIARY
or
INTELLIGENCE SUMMARY.
(Erase heading not required.)

Place	Date	Hour	Summary of Events and Information	Remarks and references to Appendices
WARLUS	30/3/17	9.30am	CRE visited 61st Co RE, 40th Infy Brigade, 11th Kings Liverpool Regt + 179th Tunnelling Co RE afterwards visited DAINVILLE workshops and 89th Co RE	
	31/3/17		CRE employed in office	

J C Barston Lt Col RE
CRE 14th Div

1577 Wt. W10791/1773 500,000 1/15 D. D. & L. A.D.S.S./Forms/C. 2118.

Vol 19

Confidential

War Diaries

C.R.E. ~~and~~ 14th Divn

~~61st 62nd 89th Field Coys~~

April 1917

B 417

A A & Q M G
14th Div

I forward herewith War diaries for April 1917 for H.Q. R.E. and the three field Cos. R.E.

5/5/17

J.C. [illegible]
Lt Col RE
CRE 14th Div

Instructions regarding War Diaries and Intelligence Summaries are contained in F. S. Regs., Part II. and the Staff Manual respectively. Title pages will be prepared in manuscript.

WAR DIARY
or
~~INTELLIGENCE SUMMARY.~~
(Erase heading not required.)

Army Form C. 2118.

H.Q. 14th Divl. RE
April 1917

Place	Date	Hour	Summary of Events and Information	Remarks and references to Appendices
WARLUS	1/4/17		61st Co: RE working in forward area with 41st Infy: Brigade (holding the line)	
			62nd Co: RE employed on Divl: work under CRE one section assisting 14th DA in preparing emplacements and O.P.s	
			89th Co: RE ~~[illegible]~~ training at DAINVILLE.	
			2 Cos: 11th Kings Liverpool Regt: Pioneers working with 41st Infy: Brigade 2 Cos: working on roads under CRE	
	2/4/17		CRE visited 41st & 43rd Infy Brigades 61st Co: RE. 11th Kings Liverpool Regt: and 179th Tunnelling Co: RE. Afterwards visited 89th Co: RE at DAINVILLE	
	3/4/17		CRE employed in office	
			Bombardment of enemy's positions commenced at 7 a.m. 2nd Lt LEWIS and BROWNE joined 62nd Co RE	
	4/4/17		CRE visited 43rd Infy: Bde and Corps Comdr. Afterwards visited 89th & 62nd Cos: RE. ARRAS shelled	
	5/4/17		CRE employed in office Bombardment continued. 2nd Lt MOORE joined 89th Co: RE.	
	6/4/17		CRE visited 41st 42nd & 43rd Infy Brigades. 61st 62nd and 89th Cos: RE. Bombardment continued	
	7/4/17		CRE employed in office	
	8/4/17		CRE visited 41st 42nd and 43rd Infy: Brigades	

1577 Wt. W10791/1773 500,000 1/15 D. D. & L. A.D.S.S./Forms/C. 2118.

Army Form C. 2118.

WAR DIARY
or
INTELLIGENCE SUMMARY.
(Erase heading not required.)

Instructions regarding War Diaries and Intelligence Summaries are contained in F. S. Regs., Part II. and the Staff Manual respectively. Title pages will be prepared in manuscript.

Place	Date	Hour	Summary of Events and Information
WARLUS	9/4/17	7.34 am	42nd & 43rd Infantry Brigades assaulted the German line and took first objective
		8.42	Above Brigades assaulted 2nd objective and took it.
		8 am	1 Section 62nd Co. RE moved forward to prepare a road for 47th Artillery Brigade to get forward to their new position
		8.30 am	2 Sections 62nd Co. RE moved forward for work as above.
		9.15 am	1 Section 61st Co. RE moved forward to reconstruct the old German tram line from the BEAURAINS-NEUVILLE-VITASSE road past TELEGRAPH HILL towards WANCOURT
		10.15 am	2 Cos. 11th Kings Pioneers moved forward to repair BEAURAINS-TILLOY road and to construct 2 tracks for pack animals north and south of TELEGRAPH HILL
		10.30 am	62nd Co. RE reported work for 47th Artillery Brigade completed.
		2.30 pm	62nd Co. RE reported all work for artillery completed
		3.30 pm	Infantry attack reported held up by machine gun fire about 1000 yds short of 3rd objective (WANCOURT-FEUCHY line)
		5.0 pm	Reserve pioneer company ordered to dig a communication trench about 500 yds long from the copse on Telegraph Hill into the Harp. This company was employed at request of 42nd I.B. on consolidating eastern edge of the Harp.

1577 Wt. W10791/1773 500,000 1/15 D. D. & L. A.D.S.S./Forms/C. 2118.

Instructions regarding War Diaries and Intelligence Summaries are contained in F. S. Regs., Part II. and the Staff Manual respectively. Title pages will be prepared in manuscript.

WAR DIARY
or
INTELLIGENCE SUMMARY.
(Erase heading not required.)

Army Form C. 2118.

Place	Date	Hour	Summary of Events and Information	Remarks and references to Appendices
WARLUS	10/4/17		2 Cos. Pioneers employed on forward tracks and road as on previous day	
			61st Co. RE continued work on tram line as before	
		1pm	89th Co. RE ordered to make good sunken road and fill in old German trenches crossing it in M5b and M6a	
			62nd Co. RE ordered to reconnoitre and prepare route for 46th and 124th Bdes RFA to their new positions N of NEUVILLE VITASSE. Reserve Co. of Pioneers to assist if required.	
			43rd IB captured portion of WANCOURT - FEUCHY line	
	11/4/17		Pioneers and RE employed as on previous day.	
			Arranged with CRE 50th Div for handing over on relief	
	12/4/17		41st Infy Brigade captured WANCOURT	
			RE Cos relieved by Cos of 50th Div. RE Cos and Pioneers moved to DAINVILLE	
			Division transferred from VII to XVIII Corps.	
	13/4/17		Pioneers & 62nd Co. RE moved to HABARCQ 89th Co. RE to MANIN 61st Co RE to BEAUMETZ	
	14/4/17		62nd Co. RE moved to LIENCOURT 89th Co. RE to SUS St LEGER	
	15/4/17		61st Co. RE moved to LE CAUROY CRE visited 61st 62nd & 89th Cos	
	16/4/17		CRE employed in office.	
	17/4/17		— do — do —	

1577 Wt. W10791/1773 500,000 1/15 D. D. & L. A.D.S.S./Forms/C. 2118.

Instructions regarding War Diaries and Intelligence Summaries are contained in F. S. Regs., Part II. and the Staff Manual respectively. Title pages will be prepared in manuscript.

WAR DIARY
or
INTELLIGENCE SUMMARY.
(Erase heading not required.)

Army Form C. 2118.

Place	Date	Hour	Summary of Events and Information	Remarks and references to Appendices
WARLUS	18/4/17		CRE visited Infy. Brigades and Field Cos. R.E.	
	19th 20th		CRE employed in office.	
	21st		CRE went to AMIENS to buy R.E. stores	
	22nd	2pm	CRE visited 61st 62nd and 89th Cos. R.E.	
	23rd		CRE employed in office. Field Cos. moved ~~to~~ with Brigade Groups to HAUTEVILLE - FOSSEUX, SAULTY and POMMIER areas	
~~BAHL~~	24th	10am.	Div H.Q. moved to BAILLEULMONT 61st Co. R.E. to BLAIREVILLE 62nd Co. R.E. to BEAUMETZ 89th Co. R.E. to BASSEUX CRE visited CRE 50th Div: ARRAS to arrange taking over 42nd Infy. Brigade moved up and relieved a brigade of 50th Div.	
BAILLEULMONT	25th	10am.	CRE visited CRE 50th Div at advanced Div H.Q. 50th Div to arrange taking over Field Cos. moved up and relieved Field Cos. of 50th Div. 41st Infy. Brigade took over ~~the~~ front line in front of WANCOURT	
"	26th		Div H.Q. moved up to advce. H.Q. (Sheet 51B. N7d 4 4.) 61st and 89th Cos employed on construction of Infy. shelters in WANCOURT and west of it. 62nd Co. R.E. wiring reserve line for 42nd I.B.	
N7d. 4.4.	27th		CRE attended Div. Conference. Pioneers moved to ARRAS	
"	28th		CRE visited 61st 62nd & 89th Cos. R.E. 3 Secns 62nd Co. R.E. allotted to 42nd I.B. and 2 Secns 61st Co. R.E. to 41st I.B. for work also 1 Co. Pioneers to each of above brigades	
"	29th		CRE visited Pioneers and inspected work on fine weather tracks being made beside BEAURAINS - TILLOY and TILLOY - WANCOURT roads. Pioneers moved to Telegraph Hill.	

1577 Wt. W10791/1773 500,000 1/15 D. D. & L. A.D.S.S./Forms/C. 2118.

Instructions regarding War Diaries and Intelligence Summaries are contained in F. S. Regs., Part II. and the Staff Manual respectively. Title pages will be prepared in manuscript.

WAR DIARY
or
INTELLIGENCE SUMMARY.
(Erase heading not required.)

Army Form C. 2118.

Place	Date	Hour	Summary of Events and Information	Remarks and references to Appendices
N7d.4.4.	30.4.17		CRE visited 61st 62nd & 89th Cos: R.E. and Pioneers.	
			J.C. Christie Lt Col RE CRE 14th Div	

1577 Wt. W10791/1773 500,000 1/15 D. D. & L. A.D.S.S./Forms/C. 2118.

CONFIDENTIAL. C.R.E.No.E.1027/2.

A.A.&.Q.M.G.,
14th (Light) Division.

Herewith War Diaries of 14th Divisional Engineers for the month of May, 1917.

[signature] Lt+Adjt R.E.
for Lieut-Colonel. R. E.
4.6.17. C.R.E. 14th Division.

CONFIDENTIAL.

Vol 20

WAR DIARIES.

14th DIVISIONAL ENGINEERS.

VOLUME 1a.

Month of

MAY.

1917.

Instructions regarding War Diaries and Intelligence Summaries are contained in F. S. Regs., Part II. and the Staff Manual respectively. Title pages will be prepared in manuscript.

WAR DIARY
or
INTELLIGENCE SUMMARY.
(Erase heading not required.)

Army Form C. 2118.

Place	Date	Hour	Summary of Events and Information	Remarks and references to Appendices
Sheet 51B N7d44	1/5/17	10am	CRE attended Divl. Conference to discuss projected attack on 3/5/17	
		2pm	Conference of Field Co Commanders to discuss forthcoming operations	
	2/5/17	3.30pm	Adjt visited work and reconnoitred roads	
		9am	CRE arranging for work of RE and Pioneers during forthcoming operations	
		1.30pm	OC 89th Co. RE came to CRE's office to get final instructions	
"	3/5/17	3.45am	Division attacked and got part of its objectives but was afterwards driven back by a counter attack to its original line.	
			At night. 89th Co. RE wired PANTHER trench 600 yds. 61st Co. RE wired the right flank of the division near WANCOURT tower. 1 Co. Pioneers carried stores for 61st Co. RE	
"	4/5/17		43rd Inf. Bde relieved 41st and 42nd Infy. Bdes in the front line. 2 Cos. Pioneers allotted to 43rd I.B. for work on communication trenches. 62nd Co. RE preparing shelters on far side of COJEUL river.	
"	5/5/17		CRE visited 43rd I.B. 61st & 62nd Cos. RE. 89th Co. RE allotted to 43rd I.B. to assist in laying out trenches etc. Work delayed at night by heavy German barrage.	
"	6/5/17		61st Co working on strong points in WANCOURT line. 62nd on shelters. 89th supervising work for 43rd I.B.	
"	7/5/17		CRE visited line of strong points with OC 61st Co RE	
"	8/5/17		Cos employed as on 6th. CRE visited Pioneers.	

1577 Wt. W10791/1773 500,000 1/15 D. D. & L. A.D.S.S./Forms/C. 2118.

Instructions regarding War Diaries and Intelligence Summaries are contained in F. S. Regs., Part II. and the Staff Manual respectively. Title pages will be prepared in manuscript.

WAR DIARY
or
INTELLIGENCE SUMMARY.
(Erase heading not required.)

Army Form C. 2118.

Place	Date	Hour	Summary of Events and Information	Remarks and references to Appendices
Sheet 51B N7d44		9.5.17	CRE visited CRE 18th Div with ref to taking over part of 18th Div front	
			CE VIIth Corps visited CRE 14th Div. Capt. JENKS relinquished appointment of adjutant to take command of 152nd Field Co. R.E. Lieut. SMELL took up duties of adjutant.	
		10.5.17	CRE attended Divl. Conference. 62nd Co. RE shelled wiring EGRET trench heavy shelling	
		11.5.17	61st Co. working on strong points in WANCOURT line. 62nd wiring EGRET trench. 89th supervising work for 43rd Infy Bde. Div. took over a portion of line from 18th Div.	
		12th	CRE visited 18th Div to discuss roads etc in area taken over. Cos. employed as before.	
		13th	Cos. employed as before	
		14th	41st Infy Brigade relieved 43rd in the line. 61st Co. RE relieved 89th Co. RE in forward area.	
		15th	No work possible on night 15/16 owing to a projected operation with gas projectors. This was postponed	
		16th	CRE visited corps line with O.C. 89th Co. RE and inspected roads	
		17th	Cos. employed as before	
		18th	Div. H.Q. moved to M 23 a 7.5 on BEAURAINS-MERCATEL road. Companies employed as before	
M23a.7.5		19th 20th	} Cos. employed as before	

Instructions regarding War Diaries and Intelligence Summaries are contained in F. S. Regs., Part II. and the Staff Manual respectively. Title pages will be prepared in manuscript.

WAR DIARY
or
INTELLIGENCE SUMMARY.
(Erase heading not required.)

Army Form C. 2118.

Place	Date	Hour	Summary of Events and Information	Remarks and references to Appendices
M23.a.7.5	21 5/17		Cos. and Pioneers employed as before.	
	22 5/17		Cos. and Pioneers employed as before	
	23 5/17		CRE went round Reserve line (A line) and parts of B and C lines with G.S.O.1	
	24 5/17		62nd Co. RE relieved 61st Co. RE. 42nd Bde relieved 41st Bde in front line. 62nd Co. RE to work under orders of Brigadier 42nd Bde	
	25 5/17		CRE went round Corps line (B+C lines) with O.C. 89th Co. RE. Some gas about from German gas shells or from our gas projectors discharged on previous night	
	26 5/17		61st Co. RE to work on new trench connecting LION and PANTHER trenches to form a defensive flank to A line. CRE visited 42nd Bde field Cos. and Pioneers	
	27 5/17		Cos. employed as before	
	28 5/17		Cos. employed as before. CRE visited field Cos. and 42nd + 43rd Bdes	
	29 5/17		Cos. employed as before CRE visited field Cos. 41st + 43rd Bdes	
	30 5/17		Cos. employed as before CRE visited CE 7th Corps	
	31 5/17		Cos. employed as before. CRE fixed site for new M.G. emp. in front of WANCOURT with G.S.O.2	

J.C. Rush[?]
Lt Col RE
CRE 14th Div.

1577 Wt. W10791/1773 500,000 1/15 D. D. & L. A.D.S.S./Forms/C. 2118.

CONFIDENTIAL.

14th Division "A".

Herewith War Diary of Head-quarters, 14th Divisional Engineers for the month of June 1917.

Lieut-Colonel. R.E.

July 1st. '17. C. R. E. 14th Division.

Vol 21

CONFIDENTIAL.

W A R   D I A R Y.

HEADQUARTERS 14TH DIVISIONAL ENGINEERS.

Volume 1b.

JUNE.

1917.

Instructions regarding War Diaries and Intelligence Summaries are contained in F. S. Regs., Part II. and the Staff Manual respectively. Title pages will be prepared in manuscript.

WAR DIARY

or

~~INTELLIGENCE SUMMARY~~.

(Erase heading not required.)

Army Form C. 2118.

HQ 14th Divl. RE
June 1917

Place	Date	Hour	Summary of Events and Information	Remarks and references to Appendices
M23a75 Sheet 51B	1.		Orders received for Lt Col. Carlin to take up appt. as CRE Corps troops 18th Corps. 61st Co. RE employed on 'A' line. 62nd Co. RE working with 42nd Infy Bde in the line. 89th Co. RE working on 'B' and 'C' lines i.e. Corps Line running just West of WANCOURT.	DSC
	2.		Tempy Lt Col. D.S. Collins DSO RE took over duties of CRE 14th Divn. Coys working as follows. 62nd Coy on front and support lines, making a trench system and wiring front of support line & COJEUL VALLEY with Bde in line. 89th Coy. work on A Line (i.e. Divl Second Line) making fire bays and wiring. 61st Coy. Work on Corps Line & running shops.	DSC
	3).		89th Coy took over work from 62nd Coy. Work continued as above.	DSC
	4th–6th		Work continued as above	DSC
	8.		56th Divn took over Northern half of line. 18th Divn took over S. half of line.	DSC
	9.		62nd Coy moved with 42nd Bde by march route to rest area.	DSC
	10.		61st Coy joined 41st Bde group in Reserve. 89th Coy and Pioneers under orders of CRE 18th Divn. HQ Divl Engrs moved to rest area at MARIEUX	DSC

1577 Wt. W10791/1773 500,000 1/15 D. D. & L. A.D.S.S./Forms/C. 2118.

Instructions regarding War Diaries and Intelligence Summaries are contained in F. S. Regs., Part II. and the Staff Manual respectively. Title pages will be prepared in manuscript.

WAR DIARY
or
INTELLIGENCE SUMMARY.
(Erase heading not required.)

Army Form C. 2118.

Place	Date	Hour	Summary of Events and Information	Remarks and references to Appendices
	11.		62nd Coy arrived at PUCHVILLERS and began training	
	12.		" " training	HC
	13		61st Coy arrived at LOVENCOURT and began training	HC
	14		" & 62nd Coy training	HC
	15		89th Coy arrived at AUTHIE and Pioneers at St LEGER	HC
	16 } 17 }		Coys training	HC
	18 } to } 21 }		61st Coy did bridging course at ORVILLE pontooning & trestle bridging. other Coys. Coy training.	HC
	22		61st Coy (dismtd) returned to LOVVENCOURT 62nd Coy (dismtd.) moved to ORVILLE	HC
	23.		62nd Coy bridging others training	HC
	24		Orders received for 3 field Coys & Pioneers to proceed by train and join 9th Corps. Training continued.	HC
	25.		62nd Coy returned to PUCHVILLERS.	HC
	26 } 27 }		training continued.	
	28		3 Field Coys and Pioneers entrained at SAULTY. H.Q. Divl Engrs remained at MARIEUX	HC
	29 } 30 }		H.Q. at MARIEUX.	HC

1/7/17

D. T. Collins
B Genl
CRE 14 Divn

1577 Wt. W10791/1773 500,000 1/15 D. D. & L. A.D.S.S./Forms/C. 2118.

SECRET.

"A" 14th (Light) Division.

Herewith the undermentioned War Diaries for July 1917,

Head Quarters R.E.

61st Field Company R.E.

62nd Field Company R.E.

89th Field Company R.E.

Capt & Adjt R.E.

1-8-17.

for C.R.E. 14th(Light) Division.

Army Form C. 2118.

WAR DIARY
or
INTELLIGENCE SUMMARY.
(*Erase heading not required.*)

Instructions regarding War Diaries and Intelligence Summaries are contained in F. S. Regs., Part II. and the Staff Manual respectively. Title pages will be prepared in manuscript.

14th Div. HQ.RE
JULY 1917
Vol 22

Place	Date	Hour	Summary of Events and Information	Remarks and references to Appendices
	1st		CRE. visited Brigades.	
	2		3 Field Coys. reported at work on the Corps line Ridge Defences opposite Wytschaete near Ypres in Belgium, digging new trenches and revetting also wiring. This work being carried out for 9th Corps second Army.	LS
	3 4		Orders received to proceed to 9th Corps Hq on 5th inst.	LS
	5		Left Marieux by Bus at 9 A.M. with Hqrs and arrived at Mont Noir (9th Corps Hq) at 6 P.M. orders received there to proceed to billets in Locre and to make Hqrs there.	LS
	6.		CRE. went round Corps line Ridge Defences with CRE 9th Corps Troops and examined the works of the Field Companies.	LS
	7.		CRE. visited Field Company Hqrs. 61st Company near Vierstraat, 62nd Company at RE Farm near Kemmel & 89th Company on Wulverghem – Wytschaete Road.	LS
	8 9		CRE visited Corps workshops at Bailleul also visited Corps Hqrs.	LS
	10 11		CRE visited St Jan's Capel the proposed Hqrs of the Division.	LS
	12 13		CRE visited Div. Staff at St. Jans Capel they having arrived there on 11th inst.	LS
	14 15		All units of 14th Division joined the 9th Corps. Field Companies making good progress with work on Corps line.	LS

1577 Wt. W10791/1773 500,000 1/15 D. D. & L. A.D.S.S./Forms/C. 2118.

Instructions regarding War Diaries and Intelligence Summaries are contained in F. S. Regs., Part II. and the Staff Manual respectively. Title pages will be prepared in manuscript.

WAR DIARY
or
INTELLIGENCE SUMMARY.
(Erase heading not required.)

Army Form C. 2118.

Place	Date	Hour	Summary of Events and Information	Remarks and references to Appendices
Ha	16.		CRE went round Ridge Defences with Col. Traill CRE 9th Corps Troops also with O.C. 62 Field Coy into his sector of the Corps line.	SS
	17		C.R.E. visited Hazebrouck 2nd Army Workshops with AA & QMG of the Division reference the manufacture of special accessories to be used in trench warfare	SS
	18.		CRE went round the camps of various battalions of the Division, also the Brigades, and arranged for certain camp improvements.	SS
	19.		CRE visited 62 Co R.E. and was visited in the afternoon by Chief Engineer of 2nd Army Major-General Glubb. RE	SS
	20.		CRE went round Corps line to see work of 61 Co RE with the O.C. of that unit he fixed finally position of certain trenches with their supporting points.	SS
	21		CRE reconnoitred back area of sector in which the Division is likely, in the near future, to operate. CRE Corps Troops asks for a "measured up" report on amount of work carried out since commencement of work on Ridge Defences (Corps line), this with a view to our handing over the works to another Division	SS SS SS
	22		CRE present at Conference at Divisional Hqrs. to discuss problems likely to be met with in the near future if the Division is called upon to take part in the assault of enemy positions. Progress of work on Ridge defences, very satisfactory. The Corps for whom we are working being very pleased	SS SS

1577 Wt. W10791/1773 500,000 1/15 D. D. & L. A.D.S.S./Forms/C. 2118.

Instructions regarding War Diaries and Intelligence Summaries are contained in F. S. Regs., Part II. and the Staff Manual respectively. Title pages will be prepared in manuscript.

WAR DIARY
or
INTELLIGENCE SUMMARY.
(Erase heading not required.)

Army Form C. 2118.

Place	Date	Hour	Summary of Events and Information	Remarks and references to Appendices
~~22~~.	22.		(cont) with the amount of work done by Field Coys.	
	23.		C.R.E. visited C.R.E 47th Division with a view to learning as much as possible about the Sector astride the Ypres-Comines Canal	LS
	24.		C.R.E. and A.A.Q.M.G. together visited HQrs. of 19th and 47th Divisions in order to learn as much as possible of our probable new sector.	LS
	25.		C.R.E. visited Companies and inspected Ridge Defences.	LS
	26.		C.R.E. visited area round the Ypres Comines Canal near the "Bluff" Crater and St. Eloi. He accompanied C.R.E. 41 Division who had just taken over from 47 Division	LS
	27.		C.R.E. saw Company Commanders, and obtained full particulars of new sector, these ~~[illegible]~~ being sent to Field Coys and Pioneers together with maps.	LS
	28.		In company with Lt Col Lewis (AAYQMG IX Div) C.R.E. visited back areas round St. Eloi in order to see the accommodation etc.	LS
SCHERPEN-BERG	29.		C.R.E. and Adjutant visited C.R.E. 19th Division and obtained from him all information re sector which we are likely to take over.	LS
WYTSCHAET.	30.		Companies finished work on Ridge Defences after completing 7000 yards of wiring in belts of 25 yards, over 1000 yards of new trenches dug and revetted with shelters and about 2500 yards of trench dug and partially completed.	LS
Locre	31	2.30	Companies rested. C.R.E.'s conference in afternoon at 2.30 PM. to decide future policies.	H Collins [illegible]

1577 Wt. W10791/1773 500,000 1/15 D. D. & L. A.D.S.S./Forms/C. 2118.

35807. W16879/M1879 500,000 3/17 R.T. (1074) Forms/W3091/3

Army Form W.3091.

Vol 23

Cover for Documents.

Nature of Enclosures.

Confidential.

War Diary

of

14th Divisional Engineers.

From 1st August 1917. to 31st August 1917.

Notes, or Letters written.

Instructions regarding War Diaries and Intelligence Summaries are contained in F. S. Regs., Part II. and the Staff Manual respectively. Title pages will be prepared in manuscript.

WAR DIARY
or
INTELLIGENCE SUMMARY.
(*Erase heading not required.*)

CRE XIV DIVN

Army Form C. 2118.

Place	Date	Hour	Summary of Events and Information	Remarks and references to Appendices
LOCRE	1-8-17		Companies resting. CRE visited Div Hq. with a view to finding out future actions.	CS
"	2-8-17		Conference at Divisional Hqrs. CRE attended all orders with regard to relieving the 41 and 19 Divisions in the Hollebeke sectors astride the Ypres Comines canal" were cancelled and the "stand to" of companies was ordered "off".	CS
	3-8-17 / 4-8-17		Orders received that Field Companies and Pioneers were placed again under orders of CRE IX Corps Troops for one day only. Companies inspected their previous work to see if any damage had been done by the weather and by shelling during the battle of the 31 July.	CS
	5-8-17		Orders received that Division would move into the Caestre area under IX Corps. Orders issued to Field Companies and Pioneers.	CS
	6-8-17		Field Companies march to Caestre leaving starting point about 12.15 PM companies having marched between 14 and 16 miles. CRE inspected companies on the line of march, the sappers marching was very good they appearing quite fresh after doing 12 miles.	CS
	7-8-17		CRE visited Pioneers and Field Companies, and warned the former to be ready to move on 8th inst into 5th Army area. Capt. Nottage R.E. of 61 Co (2nd in Command) appointed O.C. 152 Field Co 37 Division in place of 4/Major A.R.C. Jenks R.E. (Killed)	CS
	8-8-17		C.R.E. inspected 62 Field Co R.E. in full marching order. also visited 89th Field Coy.	

1577 Wt. W10791/1773 500,000 1/15 D. D. & L. A.D.S.S./Forms/C. 2118.

Army Form C. 2118.

Instructions regarding War Diaries and Intelligence Summaries are contained in F. S. Regs., Part II. and the Staff Manual respectively. Title pages will be prepared in manuscript.

WAR DIARY
or
INTELLIGENCE SUMMARY.
(Erase heading not required.)

Place	Date	Hour	Summary of Events and Information	Remarks and references to Appendices
~~[illegible]~~ Belgium	9/8/17 - 13-8-17		C.R.E. visited companies. Division Resting.	SS
	14-8-17		Orders received that Division was to move to Reninghelst in Belgium	SS
Reninghelst.	15-8-17		Division moved to Reninghelst area in 2nd Corps 5th Army.	SS
	16-8-17		Field Company Commanders sent up to reconnoitre new sector astride YPRES-MENIN RD.	SS
Dickebusch	17-8-17 / 18-8-17		14 Division relieves 56 Division and one Brigade of 18th Division in the line. Divisional Hqrs established near Dickebusch.	
	19-8-17		Field Coys and Pioneers now engaged on tracks and roads, the preparation of Dressing Stations (Advanced) and the formation of advanced dumps of Engineer Store Dumps with a view to carrying on with the advance. C.R.E. visited the line in company with O.C. 89 Field Coy R.E.	
	20/8/17		C.R.E. went round the line with A.D.M.S. and examined Dressing Station and arrangements for dealing with and evacuating wounded. Field Coys and Pioneers pushing ahead with infantry and mule tracks also the repair of main YPRES-MENIN, this road being diverted round Hooge owing to the difficulties in crossing the craters at this village	
	21/8/17		Work being pushed on at top speed hasty arrangements for dealing with the wounded; and tracks being prepared for mule transport. Work heavily	

1577 Wt. W10791/1773 500,000 1/15 D. D. & L. A.D.S.S./Forms/C. 2118.

Instructions regarding War Diaries and Intelligence Summaries are contained in F. S. Regs., Part II. and the Staff Manual respectively. Title pages will be prepared in manuscript.

WAR DIARY
or
INTELLIGENCE SUMMARY.
(Erase heading not required.)

Army Form C. 2118.

Place	Date	Hour	Summary of Events and Information	Remarks and references to Appendices
21	21/8/17		Shelled by the enemy, trenchboard tracks and YPRES-MENIN Road very badly damaged. Work was carried out on the avoiding tracks around Hooge, south of the village; a tramway, duckboard and Mule Track were made up.	LS
	22/8/17	7AM.	14 Division attacked the enemy from Glencorse Wood to South of Inverness Copse, a very strong resistance was put up by the enemy, the Division succeeded however in establishing a line in Glencorse Wood and halfway through Inverness Copse. Field Coys and Pioneers held all day in reserve. At night 61 Field Coy sent up to Brigade Hqrs a section of Sappers to strengthen dugouts, owing to heavy shelling and direct hits the Bde Hqrs dugout was in danger of collapsing.	LS
	23/8/17	7AM.	Work again resumed after 7.AM. work of 62 Field Co could not be carried on owing to heavy barrage put down by the enemy for their counter attack. Most of the work completed on tracks suffered very heavily from shell fire, the enemy making a special target of all regularly ~~tracks~~ defined tracks. Owing to operations of the Division, since arriving in the line it was only possible to put in approximately just over 3 days work. During this time communication was made close up to the front line, for infantry by duckboard tracks, and for Pack Mules by levelling the ground and laying down "mats" of rough planking and logs. A walkable track was also provided for the artillery, which proved a great boon to their transport in getting ammunition up to the Guns.	

1577 Wt. W10791/1773 500,000 1/15 D. D. & L. A.D.S.S./Forms/C. 2118.

Instructions regarding War Diaries and Intelligence Summaries are contained in F. S. Regs., Part II. and the Staff Manual respectively. Title pages will be prepared in manuscript.

WAR DIARY
or
INTELLIGENCE SUMMARY.
(Erase heading not required.)

Army Form C. 2118.

Place	Date	Hour	Summary of Events and Information	Remarks and references to Appendices
	23/8/17		6 Sappers and 2 NCO's of the 61 Field Co RE who had been detailed to accompany the assaulting Infantry, for blowing open the doors of enemy blockhouses, were returned to their unit, their services had not been called for.	L.S.
			61 Field Co. again sent up parties to strengthen a dug out for an Artillery Brigade, this had been very heavily shelled and its complete collapse was only saved in time.	
			Enemy counter attacked our Division heavily at 6 50 A.M. but was repulsed at all points.	
	24/8/17		Owing to casualties and the hopelessness of carrying out work under heavy shell fire the G.O.C. ordered work around Hooge and Sanctuary Wood to cease until the situation was quieter. Heavy enemy attacks proceeded througout the day, extremely heavy artillery fire. Situation quieter in the evening, 200 Pioneers taken for stretcher bearer duty.	L.S.
	25/8/17		C.R.E. visited Corps "Q" conference to determine Winter policy with reference to accommodation.	L.S.
	26/8/17		Normal Work in front line again resumed; information received that 23rd Division was coming up to relieve 14 Division; handing over reports were immediately prepared.	L.S.

1577 Wt. W10791/1773 500,000 1/15 D. D. & L. A.D.S.S./Forms/C. 2118.

Instructions regarding War Diaries and Intelligence Summaries are contained in F. S. Regs., Part II. and the Staff Manual respectively. Title pages will be prepared in manuscript.

WAR DIARY
or
INTELLIGENCE SUMMARY.
(Erase heading not required.)

Army Form C. 2118.

Place	Date	Hour	Summary of Events and Information	Remarks and references to Appendices
Dickebusch	27/8/17		CRE 14 Div. handed over to CRE 23rd Div. and in the afternoon moved to Reninghelst. Field Coys. moved into 2ND Corps Staging areas.	
	28/8/17		Division warned to be ready to move out of Corps area.	
	29/8/17		RE Hqrs moved to BERTHEN in FRANCE. II Anzac Corps area.	
	30/8/17		Extensive Training programme arranged for Field Companies, this included Gas Defence Lectures and Demonstrations by Divisional Gas Officer; Bombing by the Divisional Bombing Officer, and Lectures on various subjects by Officers of different companies. Companies were asked to send in names of any NCO's or men who had special qualifications in lecturing and instructing on subjects like, ~~[illegible]~~ physical training, musketry, observation etc etc.	
	31/8/17		Orders received that one Brigade of the Division was to move into the line in relief of the 90th Inf. Brigade. 30th Division. Further orders received as follows:-	
	31/8/17		-RE Hqrs to move with Divisional Hqrs to RAVELSBERG near BAILLEUL. and the 42 Inf Bde with 62 Field Co. to take over the sector between the River DOUVE and the BLAUWE POORTE BEEK. -opposite MESSINES.-	

(A7092). Wt. W12839/M1293 750,000. 1/17. D. D. & L., Ltd. Forms/C.2118/14.

Instructions regarding War Diaries and Intelligence Summaries are contained in F. S. Regs., Part II. and the Staff Manual respectively. Title pages will be prepared in manuscript.

WAR DIARY
or
INTELLIGENCE SUMMARY.
(*Erase heading not required.*)

Army Form C. 2118.

HQ RE 14 Division
62 Fd Coy

Vol 24

Place	Date	Hour	Summary of Events and Information	Remarks and references to Appendices
BERTHEN (France)	1/9/17		Orders to move to the line were received, and orders issued for the 62 Field Coy to march with the Brigade moving into the line – the 42 Inf Bde. – R.E. Hqrs moved from BERTHEN to RAVELSBERG CAMP in relief of 4th Australian Division. CRE visited 30th Division who had held the sector in which we were to go. The boundaries of this front extended from the BLAUWEPOORTEBEEK River to the River DOUVE. This being held by one Brigade in Front Line and one in support.	LS
	2/9/17.		89th Field Coy moved up into camp near WULVERGHEM alongside the 62 Co RE. On night of 2/3rd the 42 Inf Bde of 14 Div relieved the 90 Inf Bde. in the line	LS
RAVELSBERG	3/9/17		New sector in very bad state no stores, parks, workshops being organised. and no organised system of defences existed. Approaches to front line very bad although railways system was very good. CRE visited the new area with a view to programme of works. 61 Field Co, RE moved into billets near NEUVE EGLISE – DRANOUTRE Road. II Anzac Corps were relieved by 8 Corps	LS
	4/9/17			
MESSINES and GAPAARD	5/9/17		Distribution of Field Coys and Pioneers settled and definite programme laid down. (Programme of Works attached.)	LS
do	6/9/17 to 12/9/17		Work proceeding satisfactorily, although demands on RE. very heavy. 14 Div Artillery demand RE assistance and are given 2 sections of 61 Fld Coy for constructing O.P's and Gun Emplacements. CRE went round line on various days with Field Company Commanders and on 12th inst with C.E. 8 Corps	LS

(A7092). Wt. W12839/M1293. 75,000 1/17. D. D. & L., Ltd. Forms/C.2118/14.

Instructions regarding War Diaries and Intelligence Summaries are contained in F. S. Regs., Part II. and the Staff Manual respectively. Title pages will be prepared in manuscript.

WAR DIARY
or
INTELLIGENCE SUMMARY.
(Erase heading not required.)

Army Form C. 2118.

Place	Date	Hour	Summary of Events and Information	Remarks and references to Appendices
do	13/9/17 – 17/9/17		CREs and A.A.Q.M.G. Corps on scheme for winter hutting. Corps asked for materials for Hutting 2 Brigades this to include Horse Standings and all Camp fixtures. 8 Corps asked for 300 Nissen Huts of Small type. 61 Field Coy provide 2 sections R.E. for work on Hutting and 100 Infantry were attached for work with the 61 Coy.	[illegible initials]
do	18/9/17 – 21-9/17		Work in Line being pushed on with; particular attention being paid to the 2 main communication trenches the Northern Trench being ~~Fanny's Avenue~~ FANNY'S STREET and the Southern Trench NEW CROSS AVENUE. Trench Tramway System thoroughly organised and Trench Tramway Officer from Pioneer Battalion being appointed.	[illegible initials]
do	23/9/17.		89 Field Coy ordered to relieve 62 Coy REs of front line work on 26th inst. Work proceeding satisfactorily large working parties being employed by REs and Pioneers. Over 1000 men (Infantry) being employed on work ordered by Divisional General Staff in addition to these Field Coys in the line and in the Reserve & corps lines were receiving large working parties from Brigades in Support and Reserve.	[illegible initials]
do	24.		Visit of Corps Commander (8 Corps) and Conference between ~~[illegible]~~ the Corps Commander and G.O.C. 14 Division there were also present Chief Engineer 8 Corps G.S.O.1 14 Division and CREs 14 Division. ~~Notes made at the conference are attached~~. Corps Commander gave ~~these notes~~ his	[illegible initials]

(A7092). Wt. W12839/M1293. 75,000. 1/17. D. D. & L., Ltd. Forms/C.2118/14.

Instructions regarding War Diaries and Intelligence Summaries are contained in F. S. Regs., Part II. and the Staff Manual respectively. Title pages will be prepared in manuscript.

WAR DIARY
or
INTELLIGENCE SUMMARY.

(Erase heading not required.)

Army Form C. 2118.

Place	Date	Hour	Summary of Events and Information	Remarks and references to Appendices
do	24/9/17		ideas on the various problems connected with the Divisional Trench System also laying down the ideals to which all should strive to accomplish or attain	[initials]
do	25/9/17		C.R.E. held conference with R.E. Field Coys and Pioneers and the important question of Drainage was discussed. A Divisional Drainage officer was appointed his duties being to advise all units on drainage of Trenches Dugouts Battery Positions etc etc. A Drainage Map was ordered to be prepared.	[initials]
do	26/9/17		C.R.E. visited the line with O.C. Pioneer Battalion, ~~and~~ all work in hand of Pioneers was examined, work was found to be satisfactory as regards amount done but quality in respect of drainage siting was not good. Certain corrections were ordered to be made immediately	[initials]
do	27/9/17		C.R.E. visited Reserve Line in evening and pegged out new Reserve Line part of the old line being abandoned owing to bad Field of Fire	
do	28/9/17 to 30/9/17		Considerable trouble being experienced in making good drains, infantry working parties being very slow to understand the necessity of making drains of large section. Hutting progressing very satisfactory, if supply of material hold good the end of October would see most of work complete.	[initials]

(A7092). Wt. W12839/M1293. 750,000. 1/17. D. D. & L., Ltd. Forms/C.2118/14.

35807. W16879/M1879 500,000 3/17 R.T. (1074) Forms/W3091/3

Army Form W.3091.

WO 95/25[illegible]

Cover for Documents.

Nature of Enclosures.

Confidential.

War Diary

Of

14th Divisional Engineers.

From 1st October 1917 To 31st October 1917.

Notes, or Letters written.

Instructions regarding War Diaries and Intelligence Summaries are contained in F. S. Regs., Part II. and the Staff Manual respectively. Title pages will be prepared in manuscript.

WAR DIARY
or
INTELLIGENCE SUMMARY.
(Erase heading not required.)

Army Form C. 2118.

Place	Date	Hour	Summary of Events and Information	Remarks and references to Appendices
RAVELSBERG	1-10-17		CRE visited Hutting work in conjunction with O.C. 61 Field Coy.	LS
	2-10-17	2 P.M. to 2.30 P.M.	Southern Part of Divisional front visited by CRE and new G.S.O.1. Lieut-Col. Bayley - Reserve Line examined and various points connected with its construction brought to notice of Pioneers.	LS
Do	3-10-17		C.R.E. visited all camps under construction, and in company with A.A.Q.M.G. of the Division visited Pioneers.	LS
Do.	4-10-17		CRE visited Workshops and Lhasktell Camp near Neuve Eglise (28 d.t) Belgium T.15.b.	LS
	5-10-17		Orders received that the Division would be moving in the near future; handing over reports were at once got out. Later on in the day information was received that the move would take place immediately. All work was stopped with the exception of handing over parties who remained at work up to 25% of strength. Orders issued to 3 Fld Coys and Pioneers to move under orders of 41 Infantry Brigade.	LS.
	6-10-17		Field Coys moved to X Corps AREA. and orders were received for RE Hqrs to move on 7th inst to near LA CLYTTE into X CORPS AREA.	LS
	7-10-17		Hqrs. RE moved at noon from RAVELSBERG to X Corps Area with Hqrs near DICKEBUSCH at 28 N 2 c 8.5. R.E. Field Coys and Pioneers working for X Corps on plank roads between ZILLEBEKE and MENIN RD work taken over from 33rd Division.	
	8-10-17		CRE visited forward roads where Field Coys and attached units were working Chief Engineer X Corps.	

(A7092). Wt. W12839/M1293. 750,000. 1/17. D. D. & L., Ltd. Forms/C.2118/14.

Army Form C. 2118.

Instructions regarding War Diaries and Intelligence Summaries are contained in F. S. Regs., Part II. and the Staff Manual respectively. Title pages will be prepared in manuscript.

WAR DIARY
or
INTELLIGENCE SUMMARY.
(Erase heading not required.)

Place	Date	Hour	Summary of Events and Information.	Remarks and references to Appendices
9	9/10/17 11/10/17		Orders received that 14 Division was to relieve 5th Division in the sector North of the YPRES MENIN Road on night of 11-12th one Brigade relieving on night of 10/11th. On 11th inst CRE Hqrs moved to Dickebusch at H34a (Ref. Belgium Sht. 28) & joined the 14 Division.	[initials]
	12/10/17		R.E. & Pioneers of 5th Division having left & handed over work was carried on by 14 Div Engineers. Work consisting of Duckboard Tracks Mule Tracks in forward areas and the provision of accommodation for 2 battalions in the Back or Reserve Brigade area.	
	13/10/17 17/10/17		Work on duckboard tracks being pressed on over 1000 trenchboards daily being laid by 2 Field Coys working in line and the Pioneer Battn. Menin Road was cleared thro' village of Hooge as far as Clapham Junction a distance of 300 yards. This work enabled a good traffic circuit to be worked up round ZILLEBEKE - HOOGE - MENIN Road. - Trenchboard tracks being badly blown up by Shell fire	
	18/10/17 23/10/17		Duckboard Tracks continued and many repairs carried out to make good the damage caused by heavy shelling. Work of clearing and maintaining the YPRES - MENIN ROAD continued. Accomodation for Brigade in Reserve considerably increased and improved.	[initials]

(A7092). Wt. W12839/M1293. 75,000. 1/17. D. D. & L., Ltd. Forms/C.2118/14.

Army Form C. 2118.

WAR DIARY
or
INTELLIGENCE SUMMARY.
(*Erase heading not required.*)

Instructions regarding War Diaries and Intelligence Summaries are contained in F. S. Regs., Part II. and the Staff Manual respectively. Title pages will be prepared in manuscript.

Place	Date	Hour	Summary of Events and Information	Remarks and references to Appendices
	24/10/17		14th Division relieved by 5th Division. 3 Field Coys and Pioneers remained for work under C E X Corps. 14th Divisional R.E. Hd Qrs moved to Berthen.	[illegible]
	25/10/17 – 31/10/17		Work under C.E. X Corps maintaining plank roads, continuing PLUMER DRIVE SOUTH to MENIN ROAD. Clearing Menin Road HOOGE to CLAPHAM JUNCTION. Constructing Fascine Track from DORMY HOUSE.	[illegible]

[illegible]
Capt. & Adjt. R. E.
for C. R. E. 14th. Divn.

(A7092). Wt. W12839/M1293. 75,000. 1/17. D. D. & L., Ltd. Forms/C.2118/14.

Second Army G.447.
Xth Corps G.101/31/71.
14th Divn. G. S.G.875.
C.R.E. 14th Divn. E.1348.

14 Div

Chief Engineer,
Xth Corps.

With reference to Xth Corps "G".101/31/71 dated 28th October 1917.

With the exception of Operations in August for which only 4 days preparatory work was available. No Offensive Operations have been carried out by this Division recently.

In October the Division was in the Line preparatory to an offensive by another Division - the following report is based on work then done.

1. PLANK ROADS.

(a) Construction.

Where the ground is very broken up it is necessary to occasionally use fascines or planks as bearers under the stringers. There is a tendency for the whole road to slip sideways in very bad ground (when the formation is built up) and revetment is necessary but can be done after completion of the road.

(b) Rate of Construction.

Up to 100 yards have been done in one day by 1 Field Company, R.E. with 350 Infantry and 200 Pioneers carrying, the carry being 1,200 yards, but the rate varies, and occasionally only 20 yards were completed owing to shell fire.

Wagons were not employed to get material to road-head as one shell will stop all wheel traffic on a single plank road, and so stop work at road-head.

(c) Single roads with long passing places are preferred in the first instance, to be doubled as soon as possible. When the road passes through a heavily shelled point, two or more tracks, some distance apart, are preferable to one double track.

(d) Lorries should not be permitted on any single plank road unless traffic is limited to one direction.

2. Mule tracks should be made as a stage between T-B. tracks and plank roads. When material is available a single plank road is preferred which can afterwards be made into a double plank road.

The rate of construction of a mule track (which will stand traffic) is so little greater than that of a road, that it does not appear advisable to make them.

3. TRENCHBOARD TRACKS FOR MEN.

In 10 days, 8,000 yards of continuous track were laid. and in addition over 2,000 yards in loops and repairs. These tracks are of first importance for the Infantry in the Line.

A carry of 3,500 yards was necessary to get the trench-boards to the most advanced point reached by the tracks.

/4..

Marking of tracks is very necessary: 40 Luminous direction signs were put up which are sufficient for moon or bright night only, but for dark nights a continuous white tape is necessary in addition.

5. Nil.

6. Tramways might have been useful, but owing to barrage fire it is very doubtful whether a continuous line could be kept in repair for more than a few hours; in any case, it would have been too unreliable. State of the ground extremely bad and much additional labour would have to be obtained.

7. No special arrangements made.

8. Impossible to find labour or get materials up to make trenches under the shell fire to which the men were subjected.

Trench systems were not advocated by "G" Staff.

9. Roads were reconnoitred with a view to their repair.

10. During operations demands were not made on the R.E. for defensive works of any description, therefore R.E. were not called upon to supply information of this description, work of communications being considered more urgent.

11. With regard to the number of R.E. and Pioneers employed on tracks and roads - this was adequate for materials available which were only just sufficient to keep all employed.

12. Attachment of 100 Infantry to each Field Company, R.E. is advocated and is about to be done in this Division.

5.11.17.

(Sgd) D.S.COLLINS, Lieut.-Col. R.E.,
C.R.E., 14th (Light) Division.

Instructions regarding War Diaries and Intelligence Summaries are contained in F. S. Regs., Part II. and the Staff Manual respectively. Title pages will be prepared in manuscript.

WAR DIARY
or
~~INTELLIGENCE SUMMARY.~~
(Erase heading not required.)

Army Form C. 2118.

HQ RE 14 D

Vol 26 HQ 14th Div: RE

Place	Date	Hour	Summary of Events and Information	Remarks and references to Appendices
BERTHEN	1/11/17 – 10/11/17		CRE visited Field Companies and Pioneers daily. On 5th inst with exception of one section of 62 Field Coy RE working on Doring House Track, all other work in line by remainder of REs was stopped.	LS
	11/11/17		Division warned to be ready to leave X Corps area and to proceed to Tilques Area near St Omer in France. No decision regarding RE Hqrs movements received. Field Coys and Pioneers being ordered to move on 12th inst	LS
			Fld Coys moved to Vlamertinghe during afternoon of 11th inst.	
	12/11/17		RE Headquarters moved to Wizernes a village near St Omer. Field Coys RE moved to POTIZE AREA for work with 1st Canadian Corps.	LS
	13/11/17		Work on the NORTH ROAD was taken over from corresponding units of 1 Canadian Division by Field Coys of 14 Division. RE Hqrs ordered to return to Canadian Corps Area. Orders received too late to move in one day	LS
VLAMERTINGHE	14/11/17		RE Hqrs moved to a camp near Vlamertinghe (approx) ~~Ref~~ BELGIUM Sht 28 H16a5.8. Work taken over from CRE 1 Canadian Divn	LS

Instructions regarding War Diaries and Intelligence Summaries are contained in F. S. Regs., Part II. and the Staff Manual respectively. Title pages will be prepared in manuscript.

WAR DIARY
or
~~INTELLIGENCE SUMMARY.~~
(Erase heading not required.)

Army Form C. 2118.

Place	Date	Hour	Summary of Events and Information	Remarks and references to Appendices
VLAMERTINGHE.	15/11/17		C.R.E. went round the works in company with OC 61 Field Coy R.E. Work consisted of laying and making the new plank road between (28 Sht) D14b8:7 and 28 D16d4:0. this is known as the NORTH ROAD.	LS
do	16/11/17		C.R.E. was visited by Chief Engineer 8th Corps which Corps took over from 1 Canadian Corps. Total number of units working under C.R.E. 14 Div. direction 5 Field Coys, 2 Pioneer Btns	LS
do	17/11/17		C.R.E. visited Companies and made arrangements for readjusting Field Coys and Pioneers, all work at night except repairs being cancelled as little or no progress could be made in the darkness.	LS
do	18/11/17		8 Corps again readjusted work, it being necessary for 100 Field Guns to be got into position on the line below Abraham Heights	LS
	19/11/17		C.R.E. in company of R.A. Brigade commander reconnoitred the positions where it was proposed to put the 100 Field Guns below Abraham Heights and found that the original proposition put forward by Corps to be impossible as the enemy could get direct observation on the forward slopes of Abraham Heights. It was finally decided at a Corps Conference to push forward the new plank road and use that for getting the Field Guns into positions immediately in front of the road. Doubling of this road was also to be pushed forward as fast as possible. Additional labour from Corps being forthcoming the work was reorganised with a view to concentrating on this work.	LS
	20/11/17		C.R.E. accompanied General Rushton, Chief Engineer of 8 Corps on visit to forward roads.	LS

Army Form C. 2118.

WAR DIARY
or
INTELLIGENCE SUMMARY.
(Erase heading not required.)

Instructions regarding War Diaries and Intelligence Summaries are contained in F. S Regs., Part II. and the Staff Manual respectively. Title pages will be prepared in manuscript.

Place	Date	Hour	Summary of Events and Information	Remarks and references to Appendices
VLAMERTINGHE. BELGIUM.	21/11/17 – 23/11/17		1 Infantry Battn. 61 and 62 Coys RE at work on double plank road from 28 D14C 2:8 to SEINE 28 D16d. 1 Pioneer Battn 14 Division the 11th King's Regt. on maintenance. 218 Field Coy lent from 32 Division with One company of 11th South Lancs Pioneers (30 Division) constructing a bridge over the HANEBEEK RIVER. Good progress made with work but 218 Field Coy was taken off work on the bridge to construct the Spur running off the Plank Road at 28 D15 a 0.7	LS
	24/11/17		218 Field Coy and all units of 30 Division not available for works, so works had again to be readjusted. The efforts of 14 Div Engineers being concentrated on the spur of which some 150 yards required completion. This was completed by evening of 24th inst. 89 Field Coy being sent to rest area arriving on 23rd inst finally settling about 24th inst at QUELMES a small village near ST. OMER in FRANCE (Pas de Calais).	LS
	25/11/17		39 Div Field Coy and Pioneer Battn placed at CRE 14 Division disposal. they were not available before 26th inst however.	LS
	26/11/17		New Orders for reorganisation of works arranged. 61 and 62 Field Coys. to work on Plank Road from KANSAS X to SEINE doubling track and pressing forward with the single track. 234 Field Coy with Working Party of 5 Shrops Light Infantry maintaining Plank Road from ~~[struck out]~~ SPREE FARM to KANSAS X. Whilst 11th King's maintained same from SPREE FARM to BRIDGE HOUSE (running South)	LS
	27/11/17		Work being pushed on with good results, but heavy barrages caused many casualties to parties working on roads.	LS
	28/11/17		Little progress on works owing to heavy shelling.	LS
	29/11/17		Arrangements made for again altering the works. Chief Engineer VIII Corps visited — CRE. 14 Division	LS

(A7092). Wt. W12839/M1293 75,000. 1/17. D. D. & L., Ltd. Forms/C.2118/14.

Army Form C. 2118.

WAR DIARY
or
INTELLIGENCE SUMMARY.
(*Erase heading not required.*)

Instructions regarding War Diaries and Intelligence Summaries are contained in F. S. Regs., Part II. and the Staff Manual respectively. Title pages will be prepared in manuscript.

Place	Date	Hour	Summary of Events and Information	Remarks and references to Appendices
	30/11/17		The Road from KANSAS X Rds to ZONNEBEKE was to be made into a double plank road one battalion of 39 Division the 14th Hampshires and 61 Field Coy available for work on this. From 23rd inst to 30th inst Over 300 yards of new plank road with formation had been finished Over 400 yards planks relaid in road repairs. One spur for Artillery off the main road at 28 D 15 a 0 7 finished, which meant the addition of 200 yards of new road. A total of 117 ~~large~~ shell holes had been filled in. Many lorries, wagons, horses and wreckage removed from Roads and communication was continuously maintained, this was in spite of the fact that the enemy's barrage lines crossed the road in various places. Work was carried on here under very hard conditions, excavating being very, very difficult owing to the state of the ground & the mud sticking to the shovels making progress very slow. Orders also received that Royal Engineers and Pioneers of 14th Division were to rejoin their Division which was coming into the PASSCHENDALE SECTOR as the LEFT DIVISION of the VIII Corps, in relief of 8th Division.	[initials] [initials]

[signature]
Capt. & Adjt. R.E.
for C. R. E. 14th. Divn.

(A7092). Wt. W12839/M1293. 750,000. 1/17. D. D. & L., Ltd. Forms/C.2118/14.

Instructions regarding War Diaries and Intelligence Summaries are contained in F. S. Regs., Part II. and the Staff Manual respectively. Title pages will be prepared in manuscript.

WAR DIARY
or
INTELLIGENCE SUMMARY.
(Erase heading not required.)

Army Form C. 2118.

HQ RE 14 D
Vol 27

Place	Date	Hour	Summary of Events and Information	Remarks and references to Appendices
VLAMERTINGHE.	1-12-17		C.R.E. visited C.R.E. 8th Division with a view to taking over the Passchendale Sector also giving information of our work to C.R.E. 8th Division.	SS
"	2-12-17		All arrangements completed for handing over works.	SS
YPRES	3-12-17		C.R.E. 14 Div handed over all work to C.R.E. 8 Division and vice versa. Relief of 8th Div R.E. and Pioneers complete. R.E. Hqrs on Canal Bank at YPRES (near the QUAY)	
"			"Passchendale" sector held by 1 Brigade in the line one in support and one in reserve. R.E. works divided into 3 sections front, centre, and rear. Order of Companies 61, 89, 62 Field Coy. Pioneers employed on maintenance of mule tracks and repair & extensions to No 5 Track (Trenchboard). Front Field Company on duckboard tracks - repair and extension - Centre Field Company - on hutting in forward administrative area also maintenance of 1 section of a Duckboard Track, and the construction of 4 standings for transport of the forward Brigade holding the line. Back Area work carried out by the 62 Field Coy included the construction of horse standings for the artilleries of 2 Divisions. Great shortage of material prevailed throughout the month, all hutting work being badly held up.	SS.
"	10-12-17		62 Coy R.E. took over works from 89 Coy on Pack LINES at the "QUAY" in YPRES	
"	11-12-17		Corps Commander visited Hqrs R.E. and discussed defensive problems with C.R.E.	SS
"	12-12-17		61 Field Coy engaged in wiring of Defended Localities on GRAVENSTAFEL RIDGE.	SS
"	13-12-17		89 Field Coy ordered to relieve 61 Field Coy on work in the front sector.	SS
"	14-12-17		61 Field Coy took over from 62 Coy R.E. work on Pack Transport lines near the QUAY in YPRES. 62 Coy being given additional hutting works for employing the sappers thus relieved.	SS

(A7092). Wt. W12839/M1293 750,000. 1/17. D. D. & L., Ltd. Forms/C.2118/14.

Army Form C. 2118.

WAR DIARY
or
INTELLIGENCE SUMMARY.

(*Erase heading not required.*)

Instructions regarding War Diaries and Intelligence Summaries are contained in F. S. Regs., Part II. and the Staff Manual respectively. Title pages will be prepared in manuscript.

Place	Date	Hour	Summary of Events and Information	Remarks and references to Appendices
YPRES	15-12-17		C.R.E. visited all works in back areas with A.A.Q.M.G. 14 (Light) Division and O.C. 62 Field Coy. Additional accommodation for horses decided upon.	[illegible]
"	16-12-17		General Staff of Division decided to carry out large wiring schemes to protect the various ridges. 89 Coy R.E. engaged largely upon wiring Abraham's Heights a ridge west of PASSCHENDAELE. 61 Field Coy report having – when in the line – laid 1400 trenchboards and erected 1300 yards of wire.	[illegible]
"	17-12-17		2 Field Coys 61 and 89 employed on wiring of a switch from "WURST FARM" to "BERLIN". Hutting work being pressed on materials however being very scarce.	[illegible]
	18-12-17 – 22-12-17		Defence work occupied 2 Field Companies and large carrying parties for wire entanglements. Trenchboard tracks extended doubled and maintained. Shelling by the enemy during this period much quieter. In forward areas a Tunnelling Company R.E. was employed on Battalion Hqrs, and accommodation for supporting troops. Bore holes having previously been made and good ground being found.	[illegible]
	23-12-17		Relief night of Brigade interfered considerably with works no parties being available from units engaged in reliefs.	[illegible]
	24-12-17		Operation Orders received from Division to the effect that the 8th Division would take over our sector on the 27th inst. Visit of C.R.E. 8 Division re[illegible] relief.	[illegible]
	25-12-17 – 26-12-17		C.R.E. Major E. O. Alabaster (acting for Lieut: Col D.S. Collins on leave) visited C.R.E. 8 Division. Handing Over reports being prepared and visits to work which 14 Division Engineers [illegible] to be [illegible] also which 8 Div R.E. were to carry on by the 2 C.R.E.s.	[illegible]

(A7092). Wt. W12839/M1293- 75?,000. 1/17. D. D. & L., Ltd. Forms/C.2118/14.

Instructions regarding War Diaries and Intelligence Summaries are contained in F. S. Regs., Part II. and the Staff Manual respectively. Title pages will be prepared in manuscript.

WAR DIARY
or
INTELLIGENCE SUMMARY.
(Erase heading not required.)

Army Form C. 2118.

Place	Date	Hour	Summary of Events and Information	Remarks and references to Appendices
YPRES.	27/12/17		Relief of sector held by 14 Division completed. 14 Division less Artillery and Engineers departed for ST. OMER area to the village of WIZERNES. CRE 14 Division took over work on Forward Roads on 8 Corps area from CRE 8 Division. 62 and 89 Field Companies with the 11th Kings Pioneer Battalion took over from 2nd and 490 Field Companies and 22 Durham Light Infantry (Pioneers). Works Order giving list of Working Parties and Distribution of Labour made out. 61 Field Coy RE went to rest area at WATOU in BELGIUM.	[illegible]
	28/12/17		Work arranged to suit alteration in working parties. These hitherto provided by fighting troops in rest being replaced by more or less permanent Working Parties.	[illegible]
	29/12/17		CRE visits all units employed or under administration of CRE 14 Division. No less than 12 units with a total Working Strength of nearly 3000 men being thus controlled.	[illegible]
	30/12/17		Information received that Hqrs RE and Field Coys also Pioneer Battn were to rejoin the Division which was in Corps Reserve at ~~[illegible]~~ WIZERNES in the TILQUES area. Pending the arrival of the 29th Division, the 11th Field Coy of the 33rd Division were to take charge of all work on forward roads. Orders received that the Transport of RE units was to march to ZERMEZEELE.	[illegible]

(A7092). Wt. W12839/M1293. 750,000. 1/17. D. D. & L., Ltd. Forms/C.2118/14.

Army Form C. 2118.

Instructions regarding War Diaries and Intelligence Summaries are contained in F. S. Regs., Part II. and the Staff Manual respectively. Title pages will be prepared in manuscript.

WAR DIARY
or
INTELLIGENCE SUMMARY.
(Erase heading not required.)

Place	Date	Hour	Summary of Events and Information	Remarks and references to Appendices
YPRES.	31-12-17.		CRE 14 Division handed over all work to O.C 11th Field Coy. RE. Field Coy Transport moved to ZERMEZEELE and billeted there for night of 31-1-17 to 1-1-18. Weather at this time very severe, consequently the roads were very bad.	[illegible]

[signature]
Capt. & Adjt. R. E.
for C. R. E. 14th Divn.

(A7092). Wt. W12839/M1293. 75?,000. 1/17. D. D. & L., Ltd. Forms/C.2118/14.

Instructions regarding War Diaries and Intelligence Summaries are contained in F. S. Regs., Part II. and the Staff Manual respectively. Title pages will be prepared in manuscript.

WAR DIARY
or
INTELLIGENCE SUMMARY.
(Erase heading not required.)

Army Form C. 2118.

HQ RE 14 D
Vol 28

Place	Date	Hour	Summary of Events and Information	Remarks and references to Appendices
VLAMERTINGHE	1-1-18		Hqrs R.E. 14 Division closed at VLAMERTINGHE (Sheet 28 H16a 5.5) and reopened same day in ~~Saint~~ SAINT MARTIN-AU-LAERT, a small village 2 KILOS. from ST. OMER. Field Coys R.E. working in the line went by train from VLAMERTINGHE to WIZERNES. Transport of all units moving in two stages by road. Royal Engineers of 14 Division thus rejoined their Division after being detached for work on forward roads under orders of CHIEF ENGINEER VIII CORPS. Orders received that the 14 Division was to be transferred to FIFTH ARMY from the FOURTH ARMY. The move would take place on 3rd inst and 4th inst for R.E. units by trains at 3 hour intervals. Entraining STATION – ST. OMER. – detraining STATION – EDGEHILL SIDING – near DERNANCOURT. (AMIENS. SHT.) DIVISIONAL HEADQUARTERS being at MERICOURT-SUR-SOMME.	LS
	2-1-18.		Field Companies packing up, cleaning transport, and making all arrangements for the move. Hqrs R.E. informed that their train would be the nineteenth on the list leaving ST. OMER. 5 P.M. on 3rd inst.	LS
	3-1-18		Hqrs R.E. entrained at ST. OMER. STATION and departed promptly at 5 P.M.	LS
MERICOURT-SUR-SOMME.	4-1-18		After an all night journey in very severe weather arrived at detraining station 3.30 A.M. met by lorries into which all goods and stores were placed, state of roads being so bad owing to ice that horse transport had to be lightened as much as possible. After a 12 Kilometre drive in lorries Hqrs R.E. landed at billets in MERICOURT-SUR-SOMME. billets consisting of an old Farmstead.	
	5-1-18		R.E. units reported having arrived in billets. The 61 Coy. at VAUX-SUR-SOMME. 62 Coy R.E. at SUZANNE. 89 Field Coy at BRAY-SUR-SOMME.	LS

(A7092). Wt. W12839/M1293. 750,000. 1/17. D. D. & L., Ltd. Forms/C.2118/14.

Army Form C. 2118.

WAR DIARY
or
INTELLIGENCE SUMMARY.
(Erase heading not required.)

Instructions regarding War Diaries and Intelligence Summaries are contained in F. S. Regs., Part II. and the Staff Manual respectively. Title pages will be prepared in manuscript.

Place	Date	Hour	Summary of Events and Information	Remarks and references to Appendices
MERICOURT-SUR-SOMME	6-1-18		Training programmes being arranged. 61 and 62 Field Coys each detail one section complete to be placed at disposal of Fifth Army School of Instruction at TOUTENCOURT and the FIFTH ARMY SCHOOL at VADENCOURT (SNIPING SCHOOL) These sections having to fix up these schools with billets and fittings for carrying on the work of instruction in practical work	LS
	7-1-18		Each Field Coy detailed to give courses to units of Infantry in their Brigades to which they were affiliated.	LS
	8-1-18		a/CRE visited Field Coys and Pioneers, also all works being carried on by Field Coys viz. fitting up Divisional Depot Battln for training reinforcements, Signallers schools etc etc.	LS
	9-1-18		a/CRE. Major F.O. ALABASTER RE. departed to XXII Corps taking up appointment of S.O. R.E to the CHIEF ENGINEER. MAJOR E.E.V. TEMPERLEY took over duties of a/C.R.E.	LS
	10-1-18		a/CRE visited Field Coys. Arrangements made for supplying necessary articles for a Divisional CROSS-COUNTRY RACE	LS
	11-1-18		Arrangements made for rifle ranges and supply of target materials 14 Division General Staff attaching the greatest importance to the training carried out in musketry	LS
	12-1-18		a/CRE warned to be ready to go on a Course of instruction at Fifth Army School of Instruction (Infantry) and to be prepared to give a lecture to Infantry Officers attending this course on the Co-operation of RE and Infantry.	LS
	13-1-18		a/C.R.E. took round the works the new acting C.R.E. Capt E.D Alexander and handed over to this officer	LS

(A7092). Wt. W12839/M1293. 75,000. 1/17. D. D. & L., Ltd. Forms/C.2118/14.

Instructions regarding War Diaries and Intelligence Summaries are contained in F. S. Regs., Part II. and the Staff Manual respectively. Title pages will be prepared in manuscript.

WAR DIARY
or
INTELLIGENCE SUMMARY.
(Erase heading not required.)

Army Form C. 2118.

Place	Date	Hour	Summary of Events and Information	Remarks and references to Appendices
MERICOURT-SUR-SOMME	14/1/18		a/Major E. W. ORMISTON R.E. appointed to command 89 Field Coy. R.E. vice Major E. O. ALABASTER R.E.	LS
	18/1/18		Training of Field Coys being carried on, many sappers however being detached for work on behalf of other units. Brigades very pleased with Courses of Field Engineering provided by affiliated Field Coys.	LS
			Some pontooning on the River SOMME was carried out notwithstanding the ice and severe weather. a/C.R.E. visited training grounds and Companies.	
do. do.	19/1/18		Newly appointed O.C. 89 Field Co. arrived for duty.	SS
	20/1/18		Cross Country Race appointed to take place this day postponement cancelled race took place. 89 Field Coy arrived in 7th place.	SS
	21/1/18		Lieut-Col. Collins arrived from leave and took over duties of C.R.E. 2 sections of 89 Field Coy ordered to go to future Headquarters of 3rd Corps at UGNY-LE-GAY. (ref ST. QUENTIN SHT.) Operation Orders for the relief of the 62nd and 154th French Division received. Field Companies to march with Brigade Groups moving off on 22nd inst.	LS
	22/1/18		C.R.E. visited 154th French Division's Chef de Génie with a view to taking over and relieving French Field Coys.	LS
	23/1/18		Companies moving with Brigade Groups on second stage of move.	
	24/1/18		Hqrs R.E. closed at MERICOURT-SUR-SOMME and reopened at GUISCARD (ST. QUENTIN SHT). Journey down by lorries a distance of 32 miles.	LS
GUISCARD	25/1/18		Visits to Hqrs of 154 Division (French) with a view to taking over.	LS

(A7092). Wt. W12839/M1293. 750,000. 1/17. D. D. & L., Ltd. Forms/C.2118/14.

Instructions regarding War Diaries and Intelligence Summaries are contained in F. S. Regs., Part II. and the Staff Manual respectively. Title pages will be prepared in manuscript.

Army Form C. 2118.

WAR DIARY
or
INTELLIGENCE SUMMARY.
(Erase heading not required.)

Place	Date	Hour	Summary of Events and Information	Remarks and references to Appendices
GUISCARD	26/1/18		C.R.E. visited Chefs de Génie of 154 French Division and 62 French Division. Companies moving into final staging area before relief.	LS
	27/1/18		C.R.E. went round the whole of the Sectors to be occupied by the 14 Division, with G.S.O. 1 of the Division. Length of front approximately 9000 yards.	LS
	28/1/18		Hqrs R.E. moved to CLASTRES in relief of the CHEF de GÉNIE 154 French Division. Relief of French Field Coys and Pioneers completed. R.E. Parks and dumps taken over and lists of stores made out on forms in quadruplicate. Copy of Works orders attached	LS (A) LS
	29/1/18		Pumping Engines and Plants taken over, also some electric lighting plants for large sets of dugouts.	LS
	30/1/18		C.R.E. went round camps of 61 and 89 Field Coys and in company with AA & QMG visited back areas.	LS
	31/1/18		Chief Engineer 3rd Corps visited C.R.E. and discussed questions of defence, supply of material etc.	LS

[signature]
Capt. & Adjt. R.E.
for C. R. E. 14th. Divn.

31/1/18

(A7092). Wt. W12839/M1293 75,000. 1/17. D. D. & L., Ltd. Forms/C.2118/14.

(A)

SECRET.

14th Division. No. S.G. 156.

41st Inf. Bde.
42nd Inf. Bde.
43rd Inf. Bde.
C.R.E.
Q. (For information).

1. On taking over the new Divisional Front from the French the principal features that require immediate attention are the clearing, draining and trench boarding of existing communication trenches and improving the defended localities in the main defensive system.

The enormous length of communication trenches in the Divisional Sector render it quite impossible to attempt and maintain all these trenches.

2. Until the line has been more fully reconnoitred and Brigades have reported what work they consider to be the most urgent in their respective sectors, the policy to be adopted on the Divisional Front will be:-

(a). To restore the communication from the ST. QUENTIN - VENDEUIL Road forward to the line of main resistance viz. Tr.MAES - PECHINE DE ST.BRIEUC -DE RENNES - DU VERT CHASSEUR.

(b). Improvement of defended localities in the above line.

Work on the communications West of the ST. QUENTIN - VENDEUIL Road will be carried out under Divisional arrangements after the forward communications have been put into a satisfactory state.

3. The following R.E. and Pioneers will be placed at the disposal of Brigades as a temporary measure to assist in carrying out this work:-

41st Infantry Bde.	H.Q. and 3 Sections 61st Field Coy. One Coy. King's. (H.20.d).
42nd Infantry Bde.	H.Q. and 3 Sections 62nd Field Coy. One Coy. King's. (H.20.d.)
43rd Infantry Bde.	H.Q. and 2 Sections 89th Field Coy. One Coy. King's. ~~(H.20.d.)~~ (CAPONNE FARM).

When allotting work to Field Companies and Engineers, definite tasks will be allotted to each. Engineers and Pioneers will not be employed together, but any additional working parties required to assist either the Engineers or the Pioneers will be found by the Infantry.

4. The R.E. attached to Brigades will be made responsible for the upkeep of the 60 and 50 cm. trench tramways (animal traction) in their respective Brigade Areas.

A.S. Bagley Lt Col

Major.
General Staff.
14th (Light) Division.

23/1/1918.

Instructions regarding War Diaries and Intelligence Summaries are contained in F. S. Regs., Part II. and the Staff Manual respectively. Title pages will be prepared in manuscript.

WAR DIARY
or
INTELLIGENCE SUMMARY.
(Erase heading not required.)

Army Form C. 2118.

HQ RE 14 D
Vol 29

Place	Date	Hour	Summary of Events and Information	Remarks and references to Appendices
CLASTRES	1/2/18		Trenches in a very bad state owing to sudden thaw after severe frost. Work chiefly concentrated on clearing communication trenches and revetting the fire bays. Trenches very wide and deep.	LS
	2/2/18		A great deal of hutting work in hand. 2 sections of 61st and 89th Field Coy employed on this work.	LS
	3/2/18		Divisional Workshops formed at JUSSY these being controlled by a section of the 62 Field Coy. Chief Work consisted of Sanitary appliances and notice boards.	LS
	4/2/18		New Defensive Scheme received. This involved the construction of a complete new line of defence known as the "BATTLE ZONE". This line was some 2500 yards from the front system of trenches. The front line to be known as the Forward Zone. The "Battle Zone" involved a great amount of work as a complete line had to be dug with thick belts of wire in front. Work on this day was commenced. Works Officers being put in charge of all work on the 3 sectors into which the BATTLE ZONE had been divided. These officers were provided by the Field Coys.	LS LS
	5/2/18		Work on BATTLE ZONE taken in hand by Chief Engineer III Corps.	
	6/2/18		C.R.E. went to Conference of C.R.Es at BLENDECQUES near ST. OMER.	LS
	7/2/18		Observation Posts in the BATTLE ZONE commenced. Working Parties provided by C.R.A. Visits by Chief Engineer III Corps to H.qrs R.E. reference the new Defence Scheme.	LS
	8/2/18		C.R.E. visited BATTLE ZONE and inspected the Work in hand, and found things generally satisfactory.	LS
	9/2/18		C.R.E. visited the Northern Brigade Headquarters.	LS

(A7092). Wt. W12839/M1293. 750,000. 1/17. D. D. & L., Ltd. Forms/C.2118/14.

Instructions regarding War Diaries and Intelligence Summaries are contained in F. S. Regs., Part II. and the Staff Manual respectively. Title pages will be prepared in manuscript.

WAR DIARY
or
INTELLIGENCE SUMMARY.
(Erase heading not required.)

Army Form C. 2118.

Place	Date	Hour	Summary of Events and Information	Remarks and references to Appendices
CLASTRES	10/2/18		C.R.E. and Divisional Machine Gun Battn Commander together visited the BATTLE ZONE and sited positions for Machine Gun Emplacements. Information received that C.R.E. 18 Division was to take over at an early date the whole work now being carried out on the BATTLE ZONE.	[initials]
	11/2/18		OC 79 Field Coy RE 18th Division visited Hqrs with a view to taking over the works. All details of working parties and methods of works shown to him.	[initials]
	12/2/18		Work on Battle Zone handed over this day. Works Officers in charge of sectors of Battle Zone ordered to remain with new Works Officers of incoming unit, so as to make good continuity of work.	
	13/2/18		CRE went round Battle Zone with G.S.O.1.	[initials]
	14/2/18		Orders received to return the 3 sections and Works Officers in charge of Battle Zone Sectors, to their respective Coys.	[initials]
	15/2/18		Field Coys given considerable additional work, assisting Artillery to reconnoitre Artillery routes and in bridging trenches	[initials]
	16/2/18		Complete scheme for demolition of bridges (13 in all) over Canal de St Quentin sent in to Chief Engineer VII Corps. Indents for necessary explosives & demolition stores sent in at same time.	[initials]

(A7092). Wt. W12839/M1293. 750,000. 1/17. D. D. & L., Ltd. Forms/C.2118/14.

Army Form C. 2118.

WAR DIARY
or
INTELLIGENCE SUMMARY.
(*Erase heading not required.*)

Instructions regarding War Diaries and Intelligence Summaries are contained in F. S. Regs., Part II. and the Staff Manual respectively. Title pages will be prepared in manuscript.

Place	Date	Hour	Summary of Events and Information	Remarks and references to Appendices
CLASTRES.	17/2/18		Northern Divisional Boundary adjusted the 41st Infantry Brigade handing over a portion of their front to 36 Division who were on our left flank.	SS
	18/2/18		Commander-in-chief of the British Armies in France Sir Douglas Haig visited Divisional Headquarters.	SS
	19/2/18		Field Companies pressing forward with work on Strong points, wiring of villages and valleys where attacks would mostly come from. Observation Posts being made in forward system. 89 Field Coy send detachment to reconnoitre a bridge which the Germans had built in No man's Land over the River OISE near the village of "MOY".	SS
	20/2/18		Operation Orders of a precautionary nature issued these to come into force in case of attack by the enemy. The latter being expected to take place early. C.R.E. inspected important works and urged forward works considered to be of primary importance.	SS
	21/2/18		C.R.E. went to REMIGNY on visit to 89 Field Coy R.E. in afternoon visited 3 CORPS CAMOUFLAGE WORKS "HAM".	SS
	22/2/18		C.R.E. went round back areas with A.A.Q.M.G. 14 DIVISION and went into questions of providing additional accommodation for troops.	SS
	23/2/18		C.R.E. went round centre sector of Divisional Front with O.C. 62 Coy R.E. in afternoon visited RE WORKSHOPS at JUSSY.	SS

(A7092). Wt. W12839/M1293. 750,000. 1/17. D. D. & L., Ltd. Forms/C2118/14.

Instructions regarding War Diaries and Intelligence Summaries are contained in F. S. Regs., Part II. and the Staff Manual respectively. Title pages will be prepared in manuscript.

WAR DIARY
or
INTELLIGENCE SUMMARY.
(Erase heading not required.)

Army Form C. 2118.

Place	Date	Hour	Summary of Events and Information	Remarks and references to Appendices
CLASTRES	24/2/18		Warning Order received that the 18 Division would in the near future take over a portion of the Divisional front. Successful rehearsal of Bridge Demolition Scheme (see attached)	SS
	25/2/18		CRE 18 Division visited CRE 14 Division with a view to taking over on the 26th inst the southern sector of the front held by the 14 Division. Reliefs arranged, 79 Field Coy 18 Division relieving 89 Field Coy 14 Division in their billets at REMIGNY.	SS
	26/2/18		Relief of Southern Sector completed. 89 Field Coy moving into centre Brigade sector in dugouts at BENAY.	SS
	27/2/18		CRE visited all 3 Companies and in afternoon visited CRE 30 Division at HAM.	SS
	28/2/18		2 Bridges over Canal St Quentin and road and railway bridges in former southern sector handed over to 18 Division	

S Hall
Capt. & Adjt. R. E.
for C. R. E. 14th. Divn.

(A7092). Wt. W12839/M1293 75,000. 1/17. D. D. & L., Ltd. Forms/C.2118/14.

14th Divisional Engineers

C. R. E.

14th DIVISION

MARCH 1918

Attached:-

Report on work of R.E. 31st Mar-31st Apr.

Army Form C. 2118.

WAR DIARY
or
INTELLIGENCE SUMMARY.
(Erase heading not required.)

Instructions regarding War Diaries and Intelligence Summaries are contained in F. S. Regs., Part II. and the Staff Manual respectively. Title pages will be prepared in manuscript.

HQ RE 14 D
Vol 30

Place	Date	Hour	Summary of Events and Information	Remarks and references to Appendices
	21.3.18		Enemy started Bombardement about 4.30 a.m.	
		5.35 am	Order "MAN BATTLE ZONE" issued. Shelling of 14th Div Front only heavy about left Brigade Sector. JUSSY MONTESCOURT and CLASTRES also shelled.	
		6 a.m.	All communications broken except line to 41st Inf Bde. ZERO hour of enemy attack 9.40 a.m.	
		12 noon	C.R.E., Lt WALKER RE. Lt DAVIES RAMC went to JUSSY.	

(A7092). Wt. W12839/M1293. 750,000. 1/17. D. D. & L., Ltd. Forms/C.2118/14.

Army Form C. 2118.

Instructions regarding War Diaries and Intelligence Summaries are contained in F. S. Regs., Part II. and the Staff Manual respectively. Title pages will be prepared in manuscript.

WAR DIARY
or
INTELLIGENCE SUMMARY.
(Erase heading not required.)

Place	Date	Hour	Summary of Events and Information	Remarks and references to Appendices
	21.3.18		6.R.6. saw that Bridges were being prepared for demolition and that all R.E. Transport was on the S.W. side of the CROSART CANAL. 6.R.6 took charge of JUSSY defences. Stragglers collected and formed up in front of JUSSY for the defence of Bridgeheads later these parties were withdrawn and dugin on the S.W. side of the Canal (Appendix)	
			Lt DAVIES RAMC formed an aid post. It is estimated that 100 cases received first aid and that an additional 100 were evacuated.	[illegible]
		12 midnight	Div H^d Q^{rs} moved from CLASTRES to PETIT DETROIT. C.R.E. gave verbal orders to MAJOR ORMSTON R.E. to blow bridges after the last patrol passed over.	
PETIT DETROIT	22.3.18	3 a.m.	C.R.E. & LT WALKER went to PETIT DETROIT.	
			R.S.M. stood by R.E. Dump MONTESCOURT ready to burn till 6 a.m. when he retired with the rearguard Cavalry Patrol having received orders from the O/c Patrol not to fire the Dump as this would have given away to the enemy the retirement of the Division behind the canal bank.	
			R.S.M. took charge of FLAVY R.E. Dump which was heavily shelled from 11 a.m.	
			Div H^d Q^{rs} moved from PETIT DETROIT to BEAUMONT.	[illegible]
	23.3.18		R.S.M. rejoined from FLAVY dump. Div H^d Q^{rs} moved from BEAUMONT to GUIVRY. G.O.C. decided to hold line GUISCARD GUIVRY. Shovels were obtained for this.	[illegible]
	24.3.18		Div H^d Q^{rs} moved from GUIVRY to QUESMY at noon to CRISOLLES at 6 p.m. and to LAGNY at midnight 24-25.	[illegible]
			R.E. H^d Q^{rs} Transport marched from GUIVRY to NOYON and from NOYON to LASSIGNY. 7 Stragglers picked up & handed over to M.P. at NOYON.	
	25.3.18		R.E. H^d Q^{rs} Transport marched from LASSIGNY to CHIRY and CHIRY to LONGUEIL (18 stragglers). Div H^d Q^{rs} moved from LAGNY to CHIRY and CHIRY to RIBECOURT.	[illegible]

(A7092). Wt. W12839/M1293. 750,000. 1/17. D. D. & L., Ltd. Forms/C.2118/14.

Army Form C. 2118.

WAR DIARY
or
INTELLIGENCE SUMMARY.
(Erase heading not required.)

Instructions regarding War Diaries and Intelligence Summaries are contained in F. S. Regs., Part II. and the Staff Manual respectively. Title pages will be prepared in manuscript.

Place	Date	Hour	Summary of Events and Information	Remarks and references to Appendices
	26.3.18		R.E. H^d. Q^rs Transport marched from LONGUEIL to BRAISNES. Transport of 3 Field Coys at BRAISNES. Div H^d. Q^rs moved from RIBECOURT to VILLERS-sur-GOUDON.	[initials]
	27.3.18		All R.E. transport less Signals marched from BRAISNE to MOYVILLERS.	[initials]
	28.3.18		" " " " " " " MOYVILLERS to BEAUREPAIRES.	[initials]
			Sappers joined Transport at BEAUREPAIRES.	[initials]
	29.3.18		March to 5th Army Area commenced.	[initials]
			H^d Q^rs R.E. & 3 Field Coys marched from BEAUREPAIRES to NOGENT.	[initials]
	30.3.18		" " " " " NOGENT to BAZICOURT.	[initials]
			Infantry were bussed to 5th Army Area.	[initials]
	31.3.18		H^d Q^rs R.E. & 3 Field Coys marched from BAZICOURT to VILLIENNES.	[initials]

[signature]
Capt & Adjt. R. E.
for C. R. E. 14th. Div^n.

(A7092). Wt. W12839/M1293. 750,000. 1/17. D. D. & L., Ltd. Forms/C.2118/14.

REPORT ON WORK OF R.E. IN THE PERIOD 21ST. MARCH TO 6TH. APRIL.

The orders given previously were that in the event of a serious attack, the three Field Coys. less one section with each Brigade would be withdrawn into Divisional reserve, the 61st. and 62nd. Coys. at CLASTRES and the 89th. Coy. at JUSSY preparing bridges for demolition.

The suddenness of the attack on the 21st. prevented the withdrawal of the 61st. Coy. who became involved in the fighting in the RAVINE DES SAULES, but the 62nd. and 89th. Coys. concentrated at JUSSY.

Orders were issued at 8.0. a.m. to prepare all bridges for demolition. At 11.0. a.m. reports were received that the bridges at JUSSY were being shelled and the C.R.E. was sent to ensure that these were kept open. The organisation of the defence of the canal was also undertaken, the 62nd. Coy. and about 500 infantry being collected, and work was carried out in digging trenches.

At midnight 21st./22nd. the C.R.E. was instructed that the Division was to withdraw behind the Canal and that all bridges were to be destroyed when the infantry had passed over.

At 2.0.a.m. it was reported that the railway bridges 101, 102, and 108, (for which the Division was not responsible), had not been prepared and these were taken in hand.

The Divisional boundary was also extended Northwards and 3 additional foot bridges had to be destroyed. All the French explosives failed and fresh charges had to be procured and laid, but all bridges were broken by 9 a.m. 22nd.

Orders were then issued for all R.E. to be withdrawn into Divisional reserve near BEAUMONT. This was done but was not completed till 11 pm as all coys had become involved in fighting at JUSSY.

At 9 a.m. 23rd it was reported that the enemy had broken through North of CUGNY and the 61st.and 62nd Companies under Major TEMPERLEY were sent up to fill the gap, followed shortly afterwards by the 89th. Company and a party of 60 Pioneers under Major JOHNSTON who moved up in support.

No gap being found these companies were then ordered to withdraw and construct defences North of BEAUMONT which was successfully done and served as a rallying point for the Infantry as they were driven back.

On the 24th. the O's C both 62nd. and 89th Companies became casualties and orders were received by these two companies to withdraw. The origin of the order is unknown. They were met by the G.O.C. 107th Brigade who ordered them up again and attached them to his Brigade. They became involved in the Infantry fighting and were broken up. Orders were sent at 11 a.m. to Major TEMPERLEY that he and the Pioneers were placed under orders of G.O.C. 41st Infantry Brigade. At 12 noon the G.O.C. decided to hold the line GUIVRY - GUISCARD, this was then reconnoitered, tool dumps made and orders given to the Field Companies to concentrate at BUCHOIRE with a view to begining work on it. It was found im possible to extricate the Companies and orders were received for the Division to withdraw before work was commenced.

From the 25th. the 61st Company remained with 41st. Infantry Brigade and were used as Infantry, then stragglers from the 62nd. and 89th Companies were collected and the Companies reformed, but they were not used again.

The 61st. Coy. remained with the 41st. Brigade till the 29th March when all 3 Companies were concentrated at BEAUREPAIRS near PONT St MAXENCE and the 11th King's Pioneers wrer also reformed.

The Companies then proceeded by march route to VERS in the NAMPTY area, where they arrived on the 2nd. being moved on the 3rd. to AUBIGNY.

At 9.45 a.m. on the 4th. orders were received for the 11th King's to move into close support of the 43rd. Brigade and for the R.E., Companies to move into Divisional Reserve at FOUILLOY. This was done, but it was then decided that the R.E. would reconnoitre and improve the Army line running South from AUBIGNY. This was done, and at 9 p.m. the 3 Companies moved into billets in AUBIGNY. At 4.15 a.m. 5th. the Army line was manned, the 3 Field Companies being placed in reserve.

On the 5th. work was continued by the 3 Companies on the Army line, an extension covering the North being made. On the 6th, the 61st. and 89th. Field Companies with large Infantry parties were employed on wiring this line. The 62nd. Company were employed on rendering passable the approaches to the bridge at GLISY.

At 5.30 p.m. 6th April, orders were received for the Companies to be withdrawn to AMIENS.

The 11th King's had from the 4th. been used as Infantry and were withdrawn with the Brigades.

The R.E.Field Companies ceased to function as such from the 23rd to 29th and it was only the critical tactical situation which rendered this necessary. Much valuable work might have been done in the retreat after the 23rd. if R.E. had been available, but though efforts we were made it was found that the Companies were too involved in the fighting for their withdrawal to be possible, until the Division was withdrawn.

DESTRUCTION OF BRIDGES OVER CROZAT CANAL.

1. This Division was responsible for bridges 3 to 11 inclusive but not for 101, 102 or 108..

The officer who was in charge Major E.W.ORMSTON, D.S.O.,R.E. has since been wounded, but reported to me that all had been satisfactorily destroyed.

2. At 2 a.m. on the 22nd. I found that no arrangements had been made for the demolition of 101 or 102 and therefore I arranged for this, but it meant using all my emergency explosives. At the same time the Divisional Boundary was extended Northwards and 3 footbridges found untouched. These also were taken in hand.

3. With the exception of bridges Nos. 11 and 11A all bridges were prepared with French explosive, and with the exception of one charge this entirely failed. It had been tested on the 20th. and was quite alright, but the damp mist destroyed its efficiency.

4. The officer responsible for bridges 3 to 7 has since been killed, but the following reports are vouched for by officers. Guncotton being used after French explosives had failed.

Bridge No. 1 - Large gap and last seen burning freely.

" " 2 - Large gap. The first gap made with Guncotton was not satisfactory, but another charge was laid and fired with the enemy on the Eastern bank.

" " 3 - Large gap (about 20').

" " 4 - Girders right down - cut through.

" " 5 - Large gap (about 20').

" " 6 - Right down.

" " 7 - Large gap (about 20').

" " 8 - Bridge under construction, French engineers prepared this for demolition but left huriedly without firing charges. Lieut. MOORE R.E. seeing this attempted to fire the charges, but they failed. He then replaced the detonators and blew the charge, but the girders still held up by a single plate accross. He then collected all the guncotton he could and blew the bottom flanges out but the plate still held.
The bridge was not at any time passable and was uncrossable, as the large gap in the centre was bridged accross by a single plate only.

" Nos. 9 & 10 - Bridges over one lock completely destroyed and rails thrown into water (Lieut. DEVERALL M.C.,R.E.).

" " 11 & 11A. Gap first made not very satisfactory but Capt. LYON with g reat gallantry after getting fresh charges, completely destroyed this under Machine gun Fire.

5. I think th eabove is sufficient to show that the work was carried out through.

6. The report that bridges were left standing was due :-

i To the idea that the destruction of a bridge meansthe elemenation of all signs of it.

ii The first charges having mostly failed.

iii The fact that the lock gates were not blown up though the foot bridge was destroyed.

iv No. 8 bridge standing, which from the distance looked intact.

7. I have spoken to a large number of officers who held the canal bank, and in no case can I hear of the enemy attempting to use any of the bridges.

8. All footbridges were completely destroyed.

9. The R.E.Dump MONTESCOURT was prepared for firing, but was not fired by order of the O.C. Cavalry rear guard.

10. At 9.45 a.m. on the 23rd. all R.E. and Pioneers were ordered into the line to fill a gap, and from that time it was found impossible to withdraw them. Rendering further R.E. work impossible.

WAR DIARY

Headquarters,

ROYAL ENGINEERS, 14th Division.

A P R I L

1 9 1 8

Army Form C. 2118.

Instructions regarding War Diaries and Intelligence Summaries are contained in F. S. Regs., Part II. and the Staff Manual respectively. Title pages will be prepared in manuscript.

WAR DIARY
or
INTELLIGENCE SUMMARY.
(Erase heading not required.)

HQ RE 14 D

Vol 31

Place	Date	Hour	Summary of Events and Information	Remarks and references to Appendices
HEBECOURT	1/4/18		C.R.E. with Div H^d Q^rs at HEBECOURT. Inf Bdes bussed to BOVES.	
			Field Coys & H^d Q^rs R.E. (less C.R.E.) marched from VILLIENNES to FLECHY	
	2/4/18		Div H^d Q^rs moved from HEBECOURT to BOVES. 3 Inf Bdes moved into	
BOYES.			line S of LUCE: 2 Bdes in front 1 in reserve. Tools supplied to each	
			Bde but no sappers available.	
			3 Field Coys & H^d Q^rs R.E. (less C.R.E.) marched from FLECHY to YERS.	
	3/4/18		Div H^d Q^rs and C.R.E. moved from BOVES to AUBIGNY.	
			3 Field Coys dismounted marched from YERS to AUBIGNY into Divisional Reserve	
			Inf Bdes took over line from SOMME to main Road.	
			Heavy transport marched from YERS to AMIENS. H^d Q^rs R.E. & light transport	
			marched from YERS to BLANGY-TRONVILLE	
	4/4/18		Div H^d Q^rs and C.R.E. moved from AUBIGNY to GLISSY. Field Coys in Div	
			Reserve standing to at 6 a.m. Enemy attacked.	
		9.45	Orders received for Pioneers to take up position covering 43rd Inf Bde	
			Field Coys to FOUILLOY then on AUBIGNY SWITCH.	
	5/4/18		Field Coys dug in on the AUBIGNY SWITCH and then moved to BLANGY-TRONVILLE	
		7.30 p.m.	H^d Q^rs R.E. rejoined C.R.E. at Div H^d Q^rs GLISSY.	
GLISSY.	6/4/18		Field Coys constructed Batt H^d Q^rs on AUBIGNY SWITCH.	

(A7092). Wt. W12839/M1293. 750,000. 1/17. D. D. & L., Ltd. Forms/C.2118/14.

Army Form C. 2118

Instructions regarding War Diaries and Intelligence Summaries are contained in F. S. Regs., Part II. and the Staff Manual respectively. Title pages will be prepared in manuscript.

WAR DIARY
or
INTELLIGENCE SUMMARY.

(Erase heading not required.)

Place	Date	Hour	Summary of Events and Information	Remarks and references to Appendices
GLISSY.	7/4/18.		61st & 89th Coys wiring on AUBIGNY SWITCH. 62nd Coy improving road from GLISSY to Pontoon Bridge across the SOMME.	
			Div Hd Qrs moved from GLISSY to St FUSCIEN. Field Coys moved to CAGNY.	
St FUSCIEN.	8/4/18.		Transport of Field Companies, less transport being entrained, started march to refitting area under command of Capt Halley.	
St FUSCIEN.	9/4/18.		at St Fuscien.	
	10/4/18	10 a.m.	Entrained at SALEUX. 62nd & 89th Field Coys detached for work on G.H.Q. Line. Detrained at GAMACHES and marched to FEUQUIERES. C.R.E. Offr & 30 men of 61st Coy went forward by lorry to fix up Baths etc in new area.	
FEUQUIERES.	11/4/18	9 p.m.	Entrained at FEUQUIERES.	
HUCQUELIERS.	12/4/18		Detrained at MARESQUEL and marched to HUCQUELIERS. 61st Coy at WICQUINGHEM.	
	13/4/18		C.R.E. went to meet C.E. 1st Army.	
	14/4/18		C.R.E. [illegible] Rear Defences with XIII Corps Commander.	
			61st Field Coy moved from WICQUINGHEM to FONTAINE.	
	15/4/18.		61st Field Coy to MOLLINGHEM. 14th Div Hd Qrs moved from HUCQUELIERS to ECQUEDECQUES. 62nd Field Coy R.E. rejoined Division at ECQUEDECQUES.	
ECQUEDECQUES.	16/4/18.		Division cut down to one Brigade of Infantry of 4 Battalions (43rd Inf Bde) to work on "Rear Defences MOLLINGHEM – CANTRAINNE" assisted by a Portuguese Bde.	
			O.C. 61st Coy Works Officer Northern Sector with 43rd Inf Bde for Work.	
			O.C. 62nd Coy Works Officer Southern Sector with Portuguese Bde.	
		2 p.m.	Tools Delivered & work started on Northern Sector.	
	17/4/18.		C.R.E. out reconnoitring the line daily.	
		2 p.m.	Tools delivered & work started on Southern Sector.	

(A7092). Wt. W12839/M1293. 750,000. 1/17. D. D. & L., Ltd. Forms/C.2118/14.

Instructions regarding War Diaries and Intelligence Summaries are contained in F. S. Regs., Part II. and the Staff Manual respectively. Title pages will be prepared in manuscript.

WAR DIARY
or
INTELLIGENCE SUMMARY.
(Erase heading not required.)

Army Form C. 2118.

Place	Date	Hour	Summary of Events and Information	Remarks and references to Appendices
ECQUEDECQUES	18/4/18. 19/4/18.		} Work continued on Rear Defences MOLINGHEM – CANTRAINNE CRE went over line both days.	[illegible]
	20/4/18.		Work continued on line also new line CANTRAINNE – BUSNES reconnoitred by C.R.E.	[illegible]
	21/4/18		Div Hd Qrs moved to COYECQUE. Work carried on as usual also work started on CANTRAINNE – BUSNES line. CRE ~~met~~ B.G.G.S. XIII Corps at 16th Div Hd Qrs. G.O.C. went round line with C.E. XIII Corps.	[illegible]
COYECQUE	22/4/18		Hd Qrs R.E. rejoined Div Hd Qrs at COYECQUE. RSM 1 clerk and 2 Orderlies left at ECQUERDECQUES.	[illegible]
	23/4/18 – 26/4/18		Work carried on as before in Rear Defences the CRE visiting the line daily.	[illegible]
	28/4/18.		Work carried on as before	[illegible]
MOLLINGHEM	29/4/18.		Work carried on as before. 14th Div Hd Qrs G & RE Hd Qrs moved to MOLLINGHEM	[illegible]
	30/4/18		CRE reconnoitred GUARBECQUE with G.O.C. Work as usual. Portugese Field Coy reported for work.	[illegible]

[signature]
Capt. & ~~Adjt.~~ R.E.
for C.R.E. 14th. Divn.

(A7092). Wt. W12839/M1293. 750,000. 1/17. D. D. & L., Ltd. Forms/C.2118/14.

Army Form C. 2118.

Instructions regarding War Diaries and Intelligence Summaries are contained in F. S. Regs., Part II. and the Staff Manual respectively. Title pages will be prepared in manuscript.

WAR DIARY

or

~~INTELLIGENCE SUMMARY.~~

(Erase heading not required.)

H.Q. R.E. 14th Division

Vol 32

Place	Date	Hour	Summary of Events and Information	Remarks and references to Appendices
MOLLINGHEM	1/5/18.		Advanced Div Hd. Qrs and R.E. Hd. Qrs at MOLLINGHEM. 61st Field Coy at MOLLINGHEM. 62nd Field Coy at ECQUEDECQUES. Work - Construction of Rear Defences L'ECLEME - BERGUETTE Sheets 36A S.W and S.E. Labour 2nd Portuguese Inf Bde and 1 Portuguese Field Coy at ECQUEDECQUES, 1 Portuguese Batt and 1 Portuguese Field Coy at MOLLINGHEM. 89th Field Coy still detached with 4th ARMY. Lt Col LLOYD OWEN with R.E. Hd. Qrs to assist with work.	A
	2/5/18.		CRE reconnoitred GUARBECQUE with G.O.C. for forming a defended locality	
	7/5/18.		63rd & 79th Labour Coys moved CORNET BRASSART 725 Labour Coy moved CORNET BOURDOIS for work on line	
	8/5/18.		89th Field Coy R.E. rejoined (CORNET. BRASSART.) 712 Labour Coy moved CORNET BOURDOIS for work on line. Div & R.E. Hd. Qrs moved from MOLLINGHEM to ST QUENTIN.	
ST. QUENTIN.	9/5/18.		1 Portuguese Inf. Batt. [2nd Batt in reserve] left for work under C.E. 1st Army.	
	11/5/18.		G.O.C. 14th Div took over 16th Div Front. 6 a.m. - 12 pm AIRE heavily bombed.	
	15/5/18.		CRE 16th DIV handed over work and Camp at Starch Factory AIRE.	
	17/5/18.		156 & 157 Field Coys R.E. Lt Col FALCON and R.E. (C.R.E. South) attached R.E. Officers and O.R. Portuguese Engineers Infantry Machine Gunners Pioneers Heavy Gunners also R.I.P. came under 14th Div for work on MOLLINGHEM. ISBERGUES THIENNES STEENBECQUE LINE.	
	24/5/18		79th Labour Coy left	

(A7092). Wt. W12839/M1293. 750,000. 1/17. D. D. & L., Ltd. Forms/C.2118/14.

Instructions regarding War Diaries and Intelligence Summaries are contained in F. S. Regs., Part II. and the Staff Manual respectively. Title pages will be prepared in manuscript.

WAR DIARY

or

~~INTELLIGENCE SUMMARY.~~

(Erase heading not required.)

Army Form C. 2118.

H.Q. R.E. 14th Division

Place	Date	Hour	Summary of Events and Information	Remarks and references to Appendices
ST QUENTIN.	19.5.18		Lt Col FALCON DSO R.E. left to resume his duties on L of C.	
	31.5.18		Lt Col S. LLOYD OWEN DSO RE left to resume his duties on L of C.	
			157 Coy R.E. left to rejoin 16th Div.	
			Work carried on throughout the month on the LILLERS – STEENBECQUE LINE.	

1/6.

H. G. Collins
Lt Col
CRE 14 Divn

(A7092). Wt. W12839/M1293. 75,000. 1/17. D. D. & L., Ltd. Forms/C.2118/14.

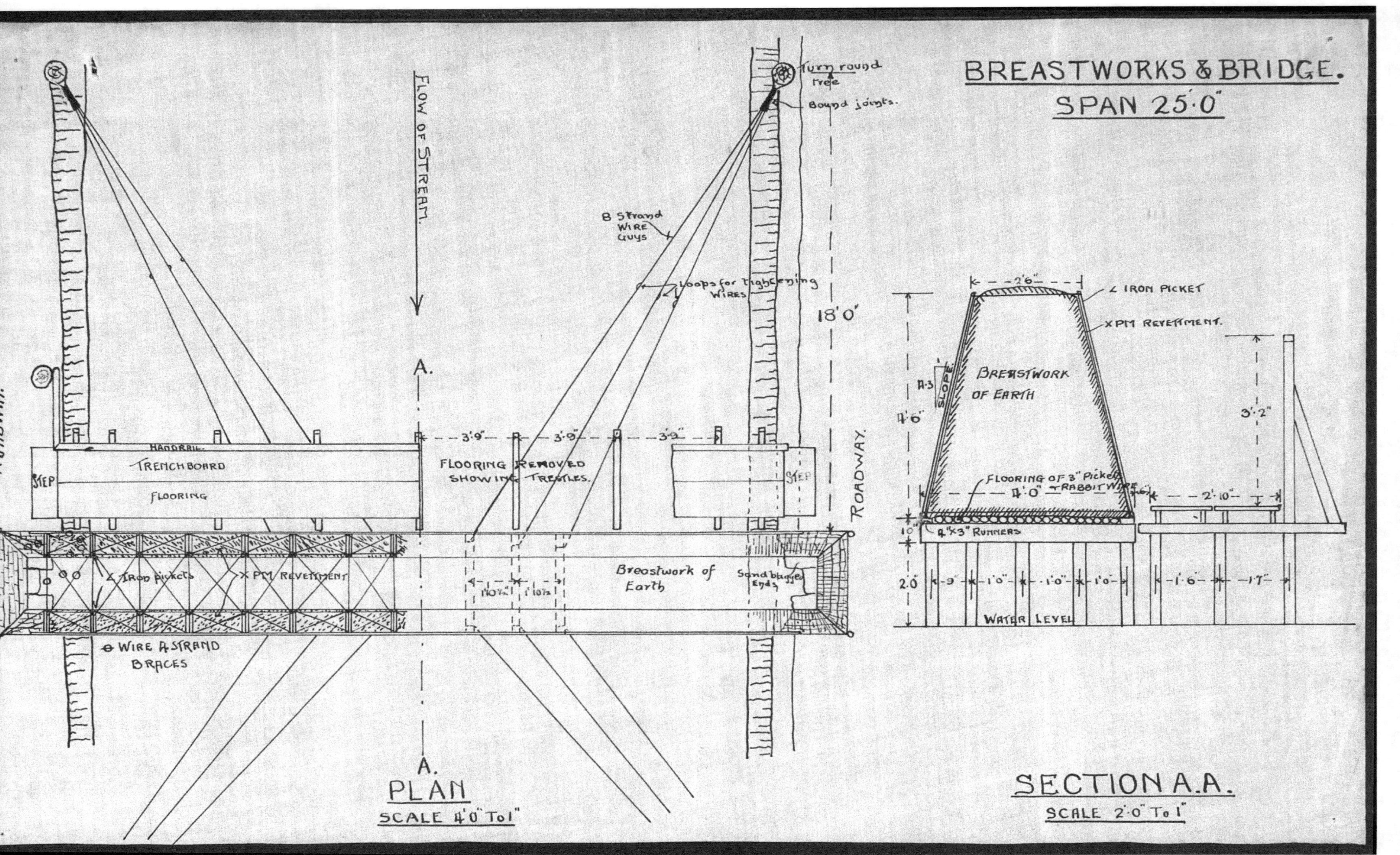

BREASTWORKS & BRIDGE.
SPAN 25'0"
Turn round tree
Bound joints.
FLOW OF STREAM.
8 Strand Wire Guys
Loops for tightening Wires
18'0"
A.
3'9"
3'9"
3'9"
HANDRAIL
TRENCHBOARD
FLOORING
STEP
FLOORING REMOVED SHOWING TRESTLES.
STEP
ROADWAY.
∠ Iron pickets
X PM REVETMENT
Breastwork of Earth
Sandbagged Ends
WIRE 4 STRAND BRACES
A.
PLAN
SCALE 4'0" To 1"
2'6"
∠ IRON PICKET
X PM REVETMENT.
BREASTWORK OF EARTH
SLOPE
4'6"
3'2"
FLOORING OF 3" Pickets + RABBIT WIRE
4'0"
2'10"
4"x3" RUNNERS
10"
2'0"
9"
1'0"
1'0"
1'0"
1'6"
1'7"
WATER LEVEL
SECTION A.A.
SCALE 2'0" To 1"

14th Div. Q.

Herewith War Diaries of 14th Divl.R.E.

Please acknowledge receipt.

Capt.& Adjt.R.E.
for C.R.E. 14th (Light) Division

July 2nd 1918

CRE 14th Div

Will you keep these till you join the Div or forward now direct to them.

[illegible] Capt for Cmdt
14th Div Details.

14th Div "G" 29

Forwarded

[illegible signature]

15/7/18

Capt. & Adjt. R.E.
for C.R.E. 14th. Divn.

Army Form C. 2118.

Instructions regarding War Diaries and Intelligence Summaries are contained in F. S. Regs., Part II. and the Staff Manual respectively. Title pages will be prepared in manuscript.

WAR DIARY
or
INTELLIGENCE SUMMARY.
(Erase heading not required.)

14th Divisional Engineers

HQ RE 14 D

Vol 33

Place	Date	Hour	Summary of Events and Information	Remarks and references to Appendices
ST QUENTIN	1/6/18.		Work on LILLERS-STEENBECQUE Defence Line. 61st Coy RE MOLLINGHEM 62nd Coy RE ECQUEDECQUES 89th Coy RE LE CORNET BRASSART. 156 Coy RE STEENBECQUE. Daily British & Portugese Labour parties of about 7000 men.	WD
	1/6/18	Noon	Came under XI Corps for supervision	WD
	2/6/18		C.E. XI Corps went round line with C.R.E.	
	6.6.18		5th R.I.R. available for work	
	8.6.18	midnight	1st Portugese Div took over administration of all Portugese Troops administered by 14th Div	WD
	10.6.18		2/4 Lon L.I. available for work.	
	11.6.18		5th Innis Fus 6th Lens Regt 5th Conn Rangers available for work.	
	12.6.18.			
	15.6.18.		14th Div HQ 24 closed at ST QUENTIN at 4 p.m. & opened Cfo Base Comdt BOULOGNE same time.	WD
			5th R.I.R. left.	
	17.6.18.		Lt Col Annesley took over command of British Troops left by 14th Div.	WD
			2/4 Lon L.I. 5th R Innis Fus and 6th Lens Regt left	WD
			C.R.E. met C.E. 1st Army & went round defence line	
	21.6.18.		Lt Col Annesley returned to XI Corps.	
	22.6.18.		Lt Col D.S. Collins commanding 14th Div Details.	
	25.6.18.		Major Stewart R.E. arrived to take over line.	
	28.6.18.		5th Connaughts left.	
			Work carried on throughout the month on the LILLERS-STEENBECQUE line. During the latter part of the month many men sick with P.U.O. which incapacitates a man from 2-4 days & leaves him rather weak.	WD

G Walker

Capt. & Adjt. R. E.
for C. R. E. 14th. Divn.

(A7092). Wt. W12839/M1293. 750,000. 1/17. D. D. & L., Ltd. Forms/C.2118/14.

Instructions regarding War Diaries and Intelligence Summaries are contained in F. S. Regs., Part II. and the Staff Manual respectively. Title pages will be prepared in manuscript.

WAR DIARY
or
INTELLIGENCE SUMMARY.
(Erase heading not required.)

Army Form C. 2118.

HQ RE 14 D

Place	Date	Hour	Summary of Events and Information	Remarks and references to Appendices
St QUENTIN.	1.7.18.		Work being carried on the construction of the LILLERS-STEENBECQUE LINE	
	4.7.18.		Major Stewart took over work on the LILLERS-STEENBECQUE LINE	
			C.R.E. Lt Col Collins on leave Major SEY TEMPERLEY acting C.R.E.	
			3 Coys working on LILLERS-STEENBECQUE LINE under Major Stewart	
	9.7.18.		61st Coy & Hd Qrs R.E. to rejoin Div. 62nd & 89th for work under VII Corps	
			61st Coy & Hd Qrs transport to SETQUES. ordered to stand fast as 14th DIV moving up.	
			62nd Coy to M.29.a. 89th Coy to G.33.a. Sheet 27	
	11.7.18.		62nd Coy and 89th Coy R.E. to St SYLVESTRE CAPPEL.	
CLARMARAIS.	12.7.18.		61st Coy R.E. rejoined the Div in EPERLECQUES area. Hd Qrs R.E. to 27/M34a.5.7.	
CASSEL.	14.7.18.		Hd Qrs R.E. to CASSEL 20th MIDDLESEX REGT arrived for work on WINNEZEELE line. 89th Coy moved to P.11.a.4.0. Sheet 27.	
	15.7.18.		33rd LONDON REGT arrived. 62nd & 89th Coy reconnoitred line.	
	16.7.18.		6th WILTS REGT arrived. Work commenced on line.	
	17.7.18.		1 Coy 15th R.N. LANCS arrived	
			Work continued on WINNEZEELE LINE (southern portion) 29.7.18 29th D.L.I relieved 33rd London Regt.	
			for work under XV Corps. 20th Middlesex left.	
	30-31		61st Coy R.E. moved to 26/C.6.c.6.5. 14th A.S.H relieved 6th Wilts. "A" Coy relieved	
	31.		89th Coy R.E. moved to LEDERZEELE	
			"B" Coy 15th R.N. LANCS.	

H. Collins Lt Col
CRE 14 D

(A7092). Wt. W12839/M1293. 750,000. 1/17. D. D. & L., Ltd. Forms/C.2118/14.

Instructions regarding War Diaries and Intelligence Summaries are contained in F. S. Regs., Part II. and the Staff Manual respectively. Title pages will be prepared in manuscript.

WAR DIARY
or
INTELLIGENCE SUMMARY.
(*Erase heading not required.*)

Army Form C. 2118.

HQ RE 14 D
Vol 35

Place	Date	Hour	Summary of Events and Information	Remarks and references to Appendices
CASSEL	1.8.18		Work being continued on the WINNEZEELE LINE southern Portion. Labour:- 62nd Coy RE "B" Coy L.N.LANCS (pioneers) 29th D.L.I. 14th A+S.H. 61st Coy R.E. attached to XV Corps for work & 89th Coy R.E. training at WESTROVE	[initials]
	11.8.18		Work ceased on WINNEZEELE LINE.	
	12.8.18		29th D.L.I. 14th A+S.H. "B" Coy 15th L.N.LANCS 62nd Coy R.E. entrained at STEENVOORDE for ST MOMELIN area. Transport by road.	[initials]
EPERLECQUES	13.8.18		C.R.E. office closed at CASSEL at 10.0 am & opened at EPERLECQUES at noon. 29th D.L.I. 14th A.S.H. "B" Coy 15th L.N.LANCS. 62nd Coy R.E. rejoined Division in EPERLECQUES area.	[initials]
	15.8.18		61st Field Coy R.E. moved by road & joined 43rd Bde Group in DROGLANDT area.	
			43rd Inf Bde Group moved to PROVEN area & were attached to 49th DIVN.	[initials]
	17.8.18		89th Field Coy R.E. joined 41st Bde Group & proceeded to WATTEN area.	
	19.8.18		62nd Field Coy R.E. joined 42nd Bde Group & proceeded to TOURNEHEM area. 61st Field Coy R.E. proceeded to MOULLE area.	
	20.8.18		Transport of Fd Coys R.E. marched to WORMHOUDT area.	
	20.8.18		C.R.E. office closed at EPERLECQUES at 10.0 am & opened at COUTHOVE CHATEAU (27/F.21.a) at the same hour.	[initials]

Instructions regarding War Diaries and Intelligence Summaries are contained in F. S. Regs., Part II. and the Staff Manual respectively. Title pages will be prepared in manuscript.

WAR DIARY
or
INTELLIGENCE SUMMARY.

(*Erase heading not required.*)

Army Form C. 2118.

Place	Date	Hour	Summary of Events and Information	Remarks and references to Appendices
CHATEAU COUTHOVE	20/8/18		89th Field Co R.E. moved by train from WATTEN to PROVEN & marched to WALKHUYSE CAMP (Sheet 27/F 25 a 29.) Transport of R.E. Coys attached to 89th Field Co R.E.	
			61st Field Co R.E. marched to camp at Sheet 28/G 4.d 7 2.)	
	28/8/18		62nd Field Co R.E. ~~entrained~~ moved from TOURNEHEM area to DIRTY BUCKET CAMP (28/A 30 central)	
	29.8.18	3 am	14th Division relieved 34 Division in the line in accordance with CRE's order No 54 (Appendix A).	
	30.8.18		61st Field Coy with 43rd Bde in Right Brigade Sector	
			62nd " " 41st " " Left Brigade Sector	
			89th Field Coy in reserve with 42nd Brigade.	[initials]

Collins
Lt Col
CRE 14 Div

Instructions regarding War Diaries and Intelligence Summaries are contained in F. S. Regs., Part II. and the Staff Manual respectively. Title pages will be prepared in manuscript.

WAR DIARY
or
INTELLIGENCE SUMMARY.

(Erase heading not required.)

Army Form C. 2118.

Headquarters 14th Div ENGINEERS

Vol 36

Place	Date	Hour	Summary of Events and Information	Remarks and references to Appendices
CHATEAU COUTHOVE	1/9/18		Div in the Line YPRES SECTOR 61st Coy R.E. working in the RIGHT BRIGADE SECTOR 62nd Coy R.E. working in the LEFT BRIGADE SECTOR.	[initials]
	2/9/18		All charges for demolitions to be withdrawn except 6 charges East of YPRES and charges at Bridge 28/I.7.c.4.7. Charges requiring a large amount of labour to withdraw & a long time to replace to be reported on before any action is taken.	[initials]
	6/9/18	9.35am	Bridge No. 6. at 28/I. 13.a.7.4 exploded cause unknown, 1 NCO & 2 Sappers killed. Report of O.C. 61st Coy R.E. attached.	[initials]
	9/9/18		Orders issued for all charges for demolitions to be withdrawn.	
	14/9/18		All charges withdrawn except Abutments of Bridge at 28/G.10.b.5.9.	[initials]
	15/9/18		89th Coy R.E. moved to ROSS CAMP.	
	16/9/18		89th Coy R.E. moved to ORWELL CAMP.	[initials]
	17/9/18		62nd Coy R.E. relieved by 90th Field Coy RE 62nd Coy DIRTY BUCKET.	
	19/9/18		61st Coy RE to G.21.b.3.4. 62nd Coy RE to H.26.c.1.9.	[initials]
ORWELL CAMP	20/9/18		89th Coy RE to H.20.a.8.4. Div Hd Qrs moved to ORWELL CAMP G.19.central. & took over part of CANAL SECTOR.	
	21/9/18 – 27/9/18		Field Coys & Pioneers engaged in making good roads mule track & bridges. Sections of 61st Coy RE moved up.	[initials]
HAGUE FARM	27/9/18 28/9/18		14th Div attacked Field Coys & Pioneers making good VOORMEZEELE – HOLLEBEKE Road: started to work at 10a.m.	
	29/9/18		Work as yesterday.	[initials]
	30/9/18		Work as yesterday.	

[signature]
Capt. & Adjt. R.E.
for C.R.E. 14th. Divn.

(A7092). Wt. W12839/M1293 750,000. 1/17. D. D. & L., Ltd. Forms/C.2118/14.

Instructions regarding War Diaries and Intelligence Summaries are contained in F. S. Regs., Part II. and the Staff Manual respectively. Title pages will be prepared in manuscript.

WAR DIARY
or
INTELLIGENCE SUMMARY.
(*Erase heading not required.*)

Army Form C. 2118.

HQ R.E. Vol 37

Place	Date	Hour	Summary of Events and Information	Remarks and references to Appendices
			14th Div Engineers. October 1918.	
HAGUE FARM	1/10/18		Divisional H.Qrs moved to WARRATAH CAMP. C.R.E. to BUSSEBOOM.	
			62nd & 89th Field Coys moved to WYSCHAETE Area 28/O 14-15-20-21.	[illegible]
BUSSEBOOM	2/10/18		Div H.Q. & CRE moved to KANDAHAR FARM. 62nd & 89th Field Coys to	
			WULVERGHEM MESSINES Area. 61st Coy R.E. to WULVERGHEM NEUVE	
			EGLISE Area.	[illegible]
KANDAHAR FM	3/10/18		9 a.m. 3 Field Coys & Pioneers came under XV Corps for work on roads.	
			62nd Coy & 2 Coys Pioneers on road East of WULVERGHEM	
			61st Coy & 1 " " on road 28/T.10.a.4.7. T/10.b.7.8. T.11.d.2.3.	
			T.18.a.4.8. T.24.A.8.9.	
			89th Coy screening road East of MESSINES.	
	4/10/18		Work as yesterday.	[illegible]
	5/10/18		Work on Roads. Screening and Div H.Qrs.	[illegible]
	9/10/18			
	10/10/18 13/10/18		Work on Roads. Making Petrol Tin Bridges & Barrel Pier Bridges.	
	14/10/18		2nd Army & Belgian Army renewed attack. 89th Field Coy put one infantry bridge across	
			the LYS. Patrols crossed but heavy shelling forced them to withdraw.	[illegible]

(A9175) Wt W2358/P360 600,000 12/17 D. D. & L. Sch. 52a. Forms/C2118/15.

Instructions regarding War Diaries and Intelligence Summaries are contained in F. S. Regs., Part II, and the Staff Manual respectively. Title pages will be prepared in manuscript.

WAR DIARY
or
INTELLIGENCE SUMMARY.
(Erase heading not required.)

Army Form C. 2118.

Place	Date	Hour	Summary of Events and Information	Remarks and references to Appendices
KANDAHAR FARM	15/10/18	0530	Attack renewed. 89th Field Coy put 3 Infantry Bridges across the LYS	
			61 & 62 Coys & Pioneers standing by.	[illegible]
	16/10/18		61st Coy RE put Pontoon Bridge across LYS at 28/X.9.b.5.9.	[illegible]
	17/10/18	1800	62nd Coy RE completed single cory bridge across LYS at 28 X central	[illegible]
	18/10/18	1235	61st Coy RE completed single cory bridge across LYS at 28/X.5.1.2	
CHAU HAZEBROUCK Q.21.C.	19/10/18		62nd Coy RE went forward with advancing Brigade.	
BLANC FOUR			Div. Hd. Qrs. to BLANC FOUR	
	20/10/18		62nd Coy RE put two infantry bridges across the CANAL DESPIERRES.	
MUSCRON	21/10/18		Div. Hd. Qrs. to MUSCRON.	
			62nd Coy put horsetransport bridge across Canal D'ESPIERRES at 37/C.7.c.83	
			Infantry reached CANAL D'ESCAUT.	[illegible]
	24/10/18		Major Holley 62nd Field Coy RE killed.	
	25/10/18		61st Coy RE relieved 62nd Coy RE with Brigade in the line. Footbridge put in at 37.C.9.c.10.	
	27/10/18		61st Coy erected footbridge at C.9.c.2.6	
	29/10/18		61st Coy erected footbridges (floating & German) at C.9.d.65.80 and at C.9.b.95.45	
	30/10/18		61st Coy put in floating Petrol Tin Bridge at C.10.a.15.14	[illegible]

[signature]

Capt. & Adjt. R. E.
for C. R. E. 14th. Divn.

(A9175) Wt W2358/P360 600,000 12/17 D. D. & L. Sch. 52a. Forms/C2118/15.

Instructions regarding War Diaries and Intelligence Summaries are contained in F. S. Regs., Part II. and the Staff Manual respectively. Title pages will be prepared in manuscript.

WAR DIARY
or
INTELLIGENCE SUMMARY.
(Erase heading not required.)

Army Form C. 2118.

HQ R.E. 14 D

Vol 38

Place	Date	Hour	Summary of Events and Information 14th Div Engineers.	Remarks and references to Appendices
MUSCRON.	1/11/18		Div Hd. Qrs at MUSCRON. 61st Coy R.E. at EYRIGNIES, working with Bde in the line.	
			62nd Coy RE at ESTAMPUIS. 89th Field Coy RE at 29/T.30.a.3.6.	[illegible]
TOURCOING	4/11/18		Div Hd. Qrs Moved to TOURCOING.	
			Bridges put over by 61st Coy RE. a Minor operation undertaken & 21 prisoners captured.	
	9/11/18		Germans retired. Pontoon Bridge put across at HELCHIN.	
			Inglis Bridge being brought down in lorries.	[illegible]
	10/11/18		2 Bridges for lorries at 37/C.9.c.2.5. completed.	
			2 Spans for lorries completed at 37/C.5.b.7.3. 9 bays Inglis bridge erected.	[illegible]
	11/11/18		Inglis Bridge being erected but slipped off launching platform.	
	12/11/18		Inglis Bridge launched.	[illegible]
	15/11/18		62nd Coy to LA MADELEINE for work under C.E. XV Corps.	
	18/11/18		61st Coy & 89th Coy to TOURCOING.	
	20/11/18		61st Coy to ESPIERRES 89th Coy to HELCHIN both for rebuilding villages.	[illegible]
	25/11/18		89th Coy RE to Tourcoing	[illegible]

[signature]
Capt. & Adjt. R.E.
for C.R.E. 14th. Divn.

(A9475) Wt W2358/P360 600,000 12/17 D. D. & L. Sch. 52a. Forms/C2118/15.

Army Form C. 2118.

Instructions regarding War Diaries and Intelligence Summaries are contained in F. S. Regs., Part II, and the Staff Manual respectively. Title pages will be prepared in manuscript.

WAR DIARY
or
INTELLIGENCE SUMMARY.
(Erase heading not required.)

HQ RE 14 D

Vol 39

Place	Date	Hour	Summary of Events and Information	Remarks and references to Appendices
			14th Divisional Engineers. Dec 1918.	
TOURCOING	1/12/18		Div Hd Qrs at TOURCOING. 61st Coy R.E. at ESPIERRES rebuilding village. 62nd Coy R.E. at LA MADELEINE working under C.E. XV Corps. 89th Coy R.E. at TOURCOING	[initials]
	3/12/18		Torchlight Tatto at ROUBAIX by 14th Div.	[initials]
	27-12-18		62nd Cy R.E. remain at LA MADELAINE but rejoin for control.	[initials]
	31-12-18		Coys employed as on 1-12-18 except 62 Cy R.E. resting.	T.J.H.J.
			31-12-18. T. G. Hutchings-Jones. LIEUT. & ~~ASST~~/ADJT. R. E. FOR C. R. E. 14 TH DIVISION.	

(A9475) Wt W2358/P360 600,000 12/17 D. D. & L. Sch. 52a. Forms/C2118/15.

Army Form C. 2118.

WAR DIARY
or
INTELLIGENCE SUMMARY.
(Erase heading not required.)

Instructions regarding War Diaries and Intelligence Summaries are contained in F. S. Regs., Part II. and the Staff Manual respectively. Title pages will be prepared in manuscript.

HQ RE 14 D
R 40

Place	Date	Hour	Summary of Events and Information — 14th Div Engineers. Jan 1919.	Remarks and references to Appendices
TOURCOING	1/1/19		Div H^d Q^rs at TOURCOING.	
			61st Coy at ESPIERES. rebuilding village.	
			62nd Coy at LA MADELEINE resting	
			89th Coy at TOURCOING building Bridge at 36/F.22.b.95.90.	
	31/1/19		and various work for Division	[initials]
			Demobilization proceeding quickly.	

[signature]
Capt. & Adjt. R. E.
for C. R. E. 14th. Divn.

(A9475) Wt W2358/P360 600,000 12/17 D. D. & L. Sch. 52a. Forms/C2118/15.

Army Form C. 2118.

Instructions regarding War Diaries and Intelligence Summaries are contained in F. S. Regs., Part II. and the Staff Manual respectively. Title pages will be prepared in manuscript.

WAR DIARY
or
INTELLIGENCE SUMMARY.
(Erase heading not required.)

Vol 41

Place	Date	Hour	Summary of Events and Information	Remarks and references to Appendices
TOURCOING	1/2/19		Div Hd Qrs at TOURCOING	
			61st Coy RE at ESPIERRES	
			62nd Coy RE at LA MADELEINE	
			89th Coy RE at TOURCOING ~~#~~ building Bridge at 36/F 22 b. 95. 90	
			+ various work for the Division.	[illegible]
	1/2/19		61st Coy RE moved to TOURCOING	[illegible]
	| 28/2/19			

[illegible signature]
Capt. & Adjt. R. E.
for C. R. E. 14th. Divn.

(A9173) W1 W2358/P360 600,000 12/17 D. D. & L. Sch. 52a. Forms/C2118/15.

Army Form C. 2118.

Instructions regarding War Diaries and Intelligence Summaries are contained in F. S. Regs., Part II. and the Staff Manual respectively. Title pages will be prepared in manuscript.

WAR DIARY
or
INTELLIGENCE SUMMARY.
(Erase heading not required.)

[RE 14 D]

[VII 42]

Place	Date	Hour	Summary of Events and Information	Remarks and references to Appendices
TOURCOING	1/3/19		Div Hd Qrs at TOURCOING	
			61st Coy RE at TOURCOING	[initials]
			89th Coy RE at TOURCOING	
			62nd Coy R.E at LA MADELEINE	
TOURCOING	9/3/19		89th Coy moved to PETIT AUDENARDE	
	8/3/19		62nd Coy moved to HERSEAUX	[initials]
TOURCOING	↓		Div Hd Qrs remained at TOURCOING	
	31st		61st Coy RE remained at TOURCOING	

[signature]
~~Capt. & Adjt. R.E.~~
for C. R. E. 14th. Divn.

(A9475) Wt W2358/P360 600,000 12/17 D. D. & L. Sch. 52a. Forms/C2118/15.

Instructions regarding War Diaries and Intelligence Summaries are contained in F. S. Regs., Part II, and the Staff Manual respectively. Title pages will be prepared in manuscript.

WAR DIARY
or
INTELLIGENCE SUMMARY.
(Erase heading not required.)

Army Form C. 2118.

HQ RE 14 D

WO 95/1843

Ceased

Place	Date	Hour	Summary of Events and Information	Remarks and references to Appendices
TOURCOING	1/4/19		Div. H^d Qrs at TOURCOING	[illegible]
			61st Coy RE at TOURCOING	
			62nd Coy RE at HERSEAUX	
			89th Coy RE at PETIT AUDENARDE.	
	to		All stores in RE Park sold to landlord living in TOURCOING.	[illegible]
	14/4/19		Lt-Col D.S. COLLINS DSO RE is struck off the strength of Hqrs RE 14 Div from 16-3-19.	
			Major E.E.V. TEMPERLEY RE (SR) 61 Fld Coy RE demobilized to England. Capt. RICHMOND commanding the Cadre of 62 Fld Coy took over command of 61 Fld Coy and Capt. L.G.M. LYON RE (TF) took over command of the 62 Fld Coy Cadre.	[illegible]
	20/4/19		CRE's Hqrs. disbanded and affiliated to Div Hqrs.	[illegible]

[illegible signature]
Major RE
a/CRE 14 Div

(A9475) Wt W2358/P360 600,000 12/17 D. D. & L. Sch. 52a. Forms/C2118/15.

www.ingramcontent.com/pod-product-compliance
Lightning Source LLC
Chambersburg PA
CBHW080904230426
43664CB00016B/2726